To All Airline Passengers

by Capt. Carlos Enrique Diaz

DORRANCE
PUBLISHING CO
EST. 1920
PITTSBURGH, PENNSYLVANIA 15222

Dorrance Publishing Co
701 Smithfield Street
Pittsburgh, PA 15222
Visit our website at www.dorrancebookstore.com

ISBN: 978-1-4809-1234-2
eISBN: 978-1-4809-1556-5

WHAT THIS BOOK IS ABOUT

- What normally happens in my airline flight?
- Answers to Airline passengers from an Airline Captain
- Airline Crew routines that most passengers should know
- Understanding Airline crew routines in your flight
- Conquer the fear of flying by knowing what is going on and why
- Much of what airline passengers want to know and have never been told.
- Things you should know as an airline passenger
- Understanding your flight as an airline passenger
- Explanations you deserve as an airline passenger and nobody told you

ABOUT THE AUTHOR

Captain Carlos Enrique Diaz was born in Venezuela in 1959, graduated as a commercial pilot in 1981, and has been an airline pilot since 1986. He became an airline captain in 1992 and for nearly three decades witnessed and still lives the advances in aviation technology and safety. All of his major experience in aviation has been in the airlines environment. At the time of writing this book, he logged more than 19,000 hours of flight in airliners, most of the time flying passengers like you around in both short and long-haul routes and domestic and international flights. Now, a United States citizen (and at the time of writing this book), he continues to be an active pilot, acting as airline captain of wide-body aircraft. He lives with his wife of twenty-seven years, his daughter, son-in-law, and two grandchildren in Fort Lauderdale, Florida.

INTRODUCTION

I have flown through the skies of four continents, being Australia the only part of the world where I have not operated.

This book was inspired by the fact that a lot of people, especially in social gatherings, when they know I am an airline pilot, ask me different kinds of questions. So, I decided to make this information available in the form of a book that you can carry with you when you fly, either on your Kindle, tablet, e-reader, or in its physical format, or you can refer to it before, during, and after a flight. Once you are done reading it, you will have information that will make flying a little more relaxing and even safer once you know the dos and don'ts and the whys.

Most of the questions I had been asked by friends, acquaintances, and passengers when they see me in uniform at the airport have been answered here.

The main objective of this book is to help you as an airline passenger have a thorough understanding of most of what is involved in every commercial airline passenger flight without having to delve into detail of the technical aspects of the flight itself.

It is necessary, though, to mention a little of the technicalities involved, but in easy-to-understand terms to help achieve the purpose of the book. For example, when you read a term in "quotes" you may refer to the "Definitions" section to know more about it. However, I will try to keep it in as much layman's terms as possible. I have included some interesting facts as well. I hope you enjoy and appreciate this content.

Although I may have not seen it all, I have seen a lot from the pilot and from the passenger perspective, and I want to share that knowledge with you as a passenger. I feel this is information you will certainly appreciate, since I have taken and continue to take regular trips as a passenger in coach and business/first class, domestic and international. Based on what I see as a passenger, but also being an active airline pilot, I can tell you a few things and make you more aware of several aspects and facts of flying as a passenger that you may have not considered or may not know about.

I believe as an experienced airline pilot, that you as a passenger will feel a lot better about flying once you go through this informative material. Regardless of the fact that you may be a frequent flyer, fly only occasionally, have not flown in years, or are looking forward to your first flight, I feel there is something for everyone in this material. If you or someone you know is afraid to fly, this information may even ease those fears. I hope you enjoy it. It's made with people like you in mind.

CHAPTER ONE

THE FEAR OF FLYING

More common these days than riding in a train and with tens of millions of people flying each year, way too many still feel that fear of defying gravity by jumping in an elongated tube fitted with wings, engines, tail, and some amenities inside to try to make us forget that we will get separated from safe grounds and soar thousands of feet above the surface, all in the name of convenience and speed to reach our destination. But for some, it is still a scary proposition as common as it is. Reasons vary, from just pure fear of heights to losing the confidence of being able to just jump outside by opening a window or a door, knowing that we are right on the surface like in a car, bus, or train. For others, there is constant fear that the plane may just fall from the sky with them inside. I have been told by some others that they don't have the sensation of being somehow in control like they may feel when they ride in a car or bus and may be able to take over, scream to the driver if something does not look right, or just plainly drive themselves and feel in complete control.

I don't possess the magic wand or the ability to dissipate completely those fears. However, my intention with this book is to at least lessen them, creating a basic understanding in simple terms of the physics of flying for one part and making sure you **are** aware of all that is involved in the execution of a commercial flight for the other. I trust that once you understand better all that is involved in a flight and particularly in a commercial flight where you are more likely to be involved in the experience of flying, you will be more relaxed and feel more confident knowing that you are actually using the safest mode of transportation when you fly.

WHAT MAKES AN AIRPLANE FLY

A lot of people are still amazed at how it is possible that an aircraft, especially the big ones, can really soar into the air and stay there for long time. The simple answer is called aerodynamics. Obviously the wings are the main components that allow an aircraft to leave the ground, as they do for birds. Bird wings were the obvious inspiration to create airplane wings. Since airplane wings cannot move up and down like bird wings to allow the aircraft to leave the ground, a different approach had to be taken. Basically the wing design allows the air below it to flow faster than the air above, thereby forcing it upwards, and that is basically what allows an aircraft to lift off the ground. The only way the air can flow above and below the wings is if we introduce speed against that air and that is why runways and engines were created. The engines propel the aircraft down the runway creating the necessary speed to allow the flow of air above and below the wings. For each aircraft, and depending on the weight at the time of takeoff, there is a minimum speed that will allow the wings to sustain flight and will allow the aircraft to take off and continue its acceleration on the air. This is also the reason airplanes take off against the wind. If the wind is flowing opposite the direction of the aircraft, also known as "headwind," it will attain its airspeed faster, or in other words, the wind speed we need to flow across the wings to perform the takeoff in the shortest distance possible. A headwind is the ideal situation during takeoff and landing. With headwind, the "air speed" is higher than the "ground speed" (see definitions). On the other hand, a tail wind is desirable during cruise flight. It will help the aircraft reach the destination faster. It explains why when you fly round trip, one segment takes longer than the other. To help you understand the concept, imagine that you are walking on one of those moving belts at the airport. If you walk on the belt and someone else is walking adjacent to you outside of the belt at the same pace in the same direction, you will still be going faster since the belt is adding speed to your direction of walking. Even though you are walking at the same pace as the person outside the belt, your speed against the fixed floor or the ground is faster. This is the equivalent of a "tail wind" on an aircraft in flight.

On the opposite, if you walk against the bell (like many children like to do for fun) and someone else is walking outside the belt in the same direction, now you are going slower than the person walking on the floor since the belt is moving in the opposite direction to where you are walking. Your ground speed is slower than the person walking out of the belt even though you may be walking at the same pace. This is the equivalent to a head-wind affecting an aircraft in flight. It will take longer to reach the destination.

AIRCRAFT MOVABLE SURFACES

In order to control its path, the airplane has movable surfaces in the tail and in the wings.

The tail contains the elevators that allow the aircraft to pitch up or down and the rudder that is vital for stabilized directional control. The elevators are the rear part of what look like small wings in the tail. When they move up with speed, the force of the wind forces the tail down and that is how an airplane commences the rotation for takeoff and can climb. When they move down, the force of the air impacting them raises the tail and creates a pitch down of the "nose," which is how the airplane descends in a controlled manner.

The surface where the elevators are located is also movable. It is called the stabilizer. It can be repositioned to make the elevators easy to operate and reduce the air loads in them.

The tail also contains the rudder, which is the movable surface in the rear of the vertical portion of the tail in an aircraft. It assists in directional control in flight and in the runway above a certain speed. Without this vertical fin and its movable surface, the aircraft would go sideways **and** out of control.

The wings contain the ailerons, the flaps, and the speedbrakes. They are slotted, movable surfaces in the wings. The ailerons on the rear part of the wing move up and down to allow the aircraft to turn in flight. Big airplanes have two separated ailerons on each wing. Smaller aircraft have only one per wing. When a right turn is desired, the aileron on the right wing moves up and the one of the left wing simultaneously moves down in the same proportion. This forces the right wing down with the air impacting the raised aileron and at the same time forces the left wing up due to the air also impacting the lowered aileron. In this manner, the airplane commences a right turn. Just the opposite occurs when a left turn is desired. The more deflection of the ailerons, the more pronounced the turns.

The flaps allow an aircraft to fly at low speeds. They extend beyond the rear and in front of the wing thereby artificially creating a bigger wing surface. They allow safe flight at slower speeds and are invariably used for approach and landing and with few exceptions in smaller planes for takeoff.

In many cases, as the aircraft approaches the destination airport, you can hear the sound of the mechanism when it activates to extend the flaps. If you are sitting by the window, you can see them moving. They are extended in stages as the speed decreases until about two to three minutes before landing, when they are completely extended to allow the slowest possible speed. Likewise, they are extended before takeoff to permit the slowest possible speed for takeoff, and as the airplane accelerates in the air, they are retracted in stages, as well, until completely retracted allowing a smoother flight at higher speeds. That is the other noise you hear a few times shortly after the wheels or "landing gear" has been retracted after takeoff.

The last surface on the wings to cover are the speed-brakes, also called spoilers. They are in the upper part of the wing and flushed with the surface and can be raised by the pilot as needed. They are most commonly used in descent and, in rare occasions, during level flight if a fast reduction in speed is required. If you have ever sat by the window, sometimes during descent you will see these movable surfaces over the wing rise. When they do, they are actually disturbing the flow of air and affecting or "spoiling" the lift of the aircraft, forcing it down. If the pilot counteracts the descent effect they create, they will cause the speed to decrease. From those facts, originates the names spoilers and speedbrakes. The most common use is to descend faster without the aircraft accelerating too much. You have probably noticed that when they are extended, the ride is not very smooth because as stated before, they disturb or spoil the smooth flow of air across the wing. But they are a useful tool for the pilot when a sharper descent is necessary, mainly because of shortcuts to the airport or to comply with instructions from Air Traffic Control (ATC).

They have another very important role during landing. Once the airplane touches down on the runway, they must be extended to spoil any remaining lift on the wings and keep the aircraft firmly on the ground. This aerodynamic action creates a downward force that increases the effectiveness of the brakes and allows the aircraft to slow down faster. These actions in combination with the engine reversers that force the air forward of the aircraft instead of backwards is what helps the aircraft slow down after landing.

Now you have a basic understanding of why and how an airplane flies. The bigger the airplane, the bigger the wings, the engines, the wheels, the brakes and the movable surfaces. It's that simple.

A CLASSIC MYTH

I would like to finish this chapter by dispelling one of the classic myths some people have about the air space. I am talking about those empty pockets of air some air travelers still believe exist, in which if the airplane inadvertently enters, it will cause it to fall suddenly. Forget about that at once and forever; there is no such thing.

What indeed exist are updrafts and downdrafts that of course will cause the aircraft not only to descend, but to climb inadvertently. We pilots are trained to know when the possibility of the existence of those drafts may occur, and we know that they are normally associated with some types of clouds, nearby thunderstorms, and mountain waves. Even though your aircraft may be flying in clear air, these updrafts and downdrafts may be experienced, especially in those circumstances or in areas where "jet streams" exist.

TURBULENCE

Turbulence or bumpy air or rough air, as we sometimes refer to it when speaking to you on the Passenger Address System or P.A., is caused by these drafts. These air currents are much more intense inside the thick clouds, which are called cumulus, and except in unavoidable circumstances during congested airspace in a terminal area or during a takeoff or landing near a thunderstorm, we pilots steer clear of these clouds. The more intense clouds, called cumulonimbus, are the ones containing intense rain, hail, and electric activity. They are a "no no" for any pilot, and we avoid them like a plague. Those are the ones that may cause severe turbulence, and we can detect them on cloudy days and at night, not only by visual clues, but by the use of the on-board radar which I will discuss in another chapter in the book.

There is also what is called "clear-air turbulence." On rare occasions there are downdrafts (or updrafts for that matter) in clear air, not associated with any of the conditions mentioned before. That is the reason why we suggest and insist that you keep your seatbelt fastened while in your seat, even though the flight is smooth, and we have turned off the seatbelt sign. Again, it's a rare occurrence, but it happens.

"Wake turbulence" is the turbulence generated by the engines of other aircraft that may be in front of ours. It is fairly common after takeoff, especially in congested airports. Air traffic controllers know about this and our concerns and try to space the takeoffs as much as possible. However, especially when taking off behind a big, heavy aircraft, those big engines generate air vortices behind them that can last for a few minutes. Obviously, the more time elapsed, the lower the effect, and it is normally felt for a few seconds. It may happen also during approach and before landing, but it's obviously less intense since the aircraft does not use nearly as much power in the engines during an approach compared to takeoff.

Less common, but existent, is the wake turbulence at high altitude. Sometimes another aircraft will cross our path at a different altitude of course, but the lower the difference in altitude, the more chance we may hit a sudden bump if the wake turbulence that aircraft left ends up in our path. It happens also when two aircrafts are on the same route at slightly different altitudes. The airplane following may be affected. In these cases, we normally get approval from air traffic control to offset our track to minimize or eliminate the situation.

For a better understanding of why the aircraft moves and shakes due to turbulence, think of the air in which the aircraft moves through like the water in a lake or in the ocean. When the air is still, it's like water in a lake or in a protected bay. If you were in a boat, it would sail smoothly. Conversely, if that same boat was in the ocean in rough waters, the ride would be shaky and even scary. It's a similar story in an aircraft, only you cannot see the air like you see the water and that is why most time when turbulence is encountered, passengers understandably get apprehensive. But there is nothing wrong, choppy or rough air, which causes turbulence, is the equivalent to choppy or rough waters. When it exists in clear air it is called "clear air turbulence." When you can see the aircraft is inside clouds, you now know turbulence is more likely to occur. Being inside thick clouds definitely resembles being on a boat on rough waters. But for your peace of mind, as a boat will sink if it gets under the water, the airplane is safer since it can drift down, up, and to the sides through the air and be able to recover its path. The farther apart from terrain, and the higher the altitude of the aircraft, the easier it is to deal with turbulence and to avoid it. When wind drafts exist near or at the airport, pilots get warned by onboard equipment, airport equipment, and reports from other pilots who previously experienced them. There are techniques we apply in these situations, and in the most severe cases, the best decision may be not to land at or takeoff from that airport.

Modern passenger and business jets designs often now include wing tip devices (the wing tips look like they are bent upward) that reduce wake turbulence and improve fuel economy.

CHAPTER TWO

YOUR FLIGHT CREW

One of the first things you should know is that every pilot, before being allowed in the cockpit of an airliner, must go through intense training that is comprised of theory, getting familiar with the type of airplane he or she will be operating, and doing extensive practice in a "flight simulator."

Every pilot—and the term pilot means both, "captain" and "first officer"—must demonstrate complete proficiency in dealing with all conceivable problems potentially encountered in a cockpit. As part of this training, the ability to work as a team is evaluated since it is of utmost importance that the pilots work in a coordinated matter. This is why all airlines have their own written standard operating procedures or "SOP," by which all crew members must abide. This, of course, does not preclude the captain from exercising his or her authority to deal with an abnormal situation in the way he or she considers the best and safest course of action.

WHAT ARE AIRLINE PILOTS TRAINED TO DEAL WITH?

- Engine failures
- Engine fires
- Engine malfunctions
- Electric, hydraulic, or pneumatic problems. Some of the systems of the aircraft are activated electrically, others through hydraulic systems, and others with air pressure (pneumatic). Most of the aircraft systems have back-up systems.
- Depressurizations: slow or sudden.

- Bad weather
- Turbulence
- Approaching and landing at an airport in low visibility or not too good weather conditions
- Partner-pilot incapacitation
- "Diversions"
- In-flight emergencies
- Aborting the takeoff and/or the landing due to different safety-related reasons. Whenever your pilot aborts the takeoff or performs a "go-around" and does not land the aircraft, rest assured, she or he is doing it for a good reason related to safety. Do not be alarmed since this was the safest course of action, and an explanation will follow once your pilots take care of the immediate duties required after doing a go-around. Relax and be patient. - - After you have finished reading this book, I know you will be.
- "Aircraft upsets" (See definitions)
- Security procedures
- Hijacking and terrorist situations

WHAT ARE CABIN ATTENDANTS TRAINED TO DEAL WITH?

- Emergency landings on ground or water called "ditching."
- Other emergency procedures
- Operating emergency equipment
- How to take care of you and guide you and your fellow passengers to safety in an emergency situation
- Fire fighting
- Unruly passengers
- Rapid depressurizations
- Sick passengers and medical emergencies
- First aid
- Death of a passenger while in flight
- Security procedures

- Hijacking and terrorist situations
- Ah, yes, serving drinks and meals, too
- Collecting payment from passengers for not covered items, like some alcoholic beverages and onboard duty free items
- Most of them can smile nicely without extra training.

The primary role of a flight attendant is to make sure that flight security and safety regulations are followed. In most countries, local aviation authorities and regulating agencies require all flight attendants to be certified for the type of aircraft where they work. I hate the fact that some passengers look at them as servants and mistreat them. They are highly trained professionals who are there mainly to guarantee your safety, and their secondary role, which most of them take very seriously, is to make sure you have an enjoyable and less stressful flight. Their job is not as easy as it seems, and they have been through a lot to be on your aircraft as a cabin attendant. They deserve the highest respect and consideration.

CHAPTER THREE

YOUR FLIGHT
WHAT ARE MY PILOTS DOING
BEFORE AND WHILE I BOARD MY FLIGHT?

First of all, normally even before getting on the airplane, the pilots meet in a room where all the associated documentation regarding the safety of the flight is assembled and prepared for them. It is also normal that out of their normal bases or when receiving an aircraft just arriving, they get all these documents at the gate and review them there, sometimes in view of all the passengers. Also, they may be delivered to them directly in the cockpit of the aircraft. The important fact is that this documentation is thoroughly reviewed by the pilots, either at the dispatch office, at the gate, or inside the cockpit.

What is in these documents?

A flight plan that indicates the route to fly, prepared normally by a team of licensed dispatchers, considering mainly weather in route, airspaces to be flying over on international routes, and of course, the fastest possible route to your destination.

A weather package that contains information about the expected weather en-route, including pictorials and satellite pictures so that the pilots can know when to expect turbulence, if any, or if the flight will be mainly smooth. Normally when there are known storms, the dispatchers prepare the route to avoid them.

Weather forecast at destination airport in a time frame that goes well before arrival time until well past estimated arrival time.

Information on possible alternate airports on the route in case a "diversion" is needed due to weather, technical issues, or a sick person on board, and at least one destination alternate airport in case that for any reason, the intended destination airport cannot be reached.

THE "WALK AROUND"

Invariably, one of the pilots will perform a walk around the aircraft before every flight. In some airliners it is customary that the copilots do it, in others, the captain will be doing it, and yet in others, the captain will make the decision on who does it. Regardless of which one of the pilots performs this exterior inspection, he or she will make sure that everything looks good. If we see something we don't like or have doubts about it, we will summon the maintenance department or the mechanic in charge and request clarification or that a defective item discovered be fixed or be put in compliance with regulations. Rest assured as a passenger that all airlines have maintenance personnel who tend to the aircraft after every arrival and before every departure.

We pilots have a logbook where we write anything we notice in flight for maintenance to take care of it after arrival (on top of the normal servicing after every flight). If we notice something abnormal during the walk around, we document it as well in the maintenance logbook. The aircraft cannot be dispatched until the item is taken care of by maintenance and a maintenance supervisor stamps his or her signature on the book, certifying that the item has been fixed or temporarily deferred if it is not critical for the operation and does not affect in any way the safety of the aircraft. Of course, both pilots must agree that it is safe to fly the aircraft when an item is not fixed right away.

Normal servicing after every landing is comprised of checking and replenishing the oil, hydraulic fluids, checking the tires, brakes, and inspecting the aircraft in general. A signature by maintenance and by the captain is required every time.

THE FLIGHT PLAN

The flight plan is a legal document prepared for every flight that contains, among many other things, the minimum fuel required for the flight, the route of the flight, expected altitudes to fly, and some other information for the pilots. We pilots always review the flight plan to make final decisions regarding fuel, route, and altitudes to ensure the most economical and efficient flight.

THE NECESSARY AND MINIMUM FUEL ON BOARD

As a passenger in an airline, be comforted by the fact that by regulations, the minimum fuel on board is more than what is needed to just fly to your destination. We review the minimum fuel required for the trip, and if for some reason we think we need even more, our professional opinion is accepted, and we have the final say in the fuel amount. We can always increase the amount, but never decrease it below the minimum required by regulations. Those regulations require that on average, we carry fuel to fly to our destination, to keep flying for another 30 minutes, and have enough to fly to another previously planned airport in case we cannot land at the destination airport.

CHECKING THE STATUS OF THE AIRCRAFT

While one of the pilots performs the walk around or external inspection, the other is checking inside the cockpit, configuring every system for flight. Another important part of the flight preparation is to check the maintenance logbook where the pilots who previously flew the aircraft may have written down any possible items that need attention by maintenance. Regardless of the fact that there was a maintenance report or not, before every departure, the maintenance logbook needs to be signed by the mechanic who serviced the aircraft, and if work was performed, depending on it, a maintenance supervisor signature is also required.

Every item, if the previous crew wrote any in the book, requires an action and response by the maintenance team.

We captains have the final authority to accept or reject an aircraft if, in our opinion, it is not one hundred percent safe for the flight.

TEAM WORK WITH THE FLIGHT ATTENDANTS: THE COMMON "BRIEFING"

We work as an integrate crew with the cabin attendants. Either before boarding the airplane or onboard before passengers enter the aircraft, we do a "briefing" or discussion together introducing each other and reviewing our normal and non-normal procedures. Good communication among crewmembers is paramount. The cabin attendants meet first and have their own briefing. Later, at some point before boarding, the pilots and the cabin attendants get together and exchange information. That is how cabin attendants find out about flight time and altitude and then pass that information to the passengers.

OTHER PREPARATIONS

Continuing with the preflight preparations, we have to calculate the performance, or in simple terms, calculate according to the weight of the aircraft, the length of runway needed for takeoff, the minimum speeds for takeoff, and other data. In order to do that we must obtain from radio automated message or from the control tower information on wind direction and velocity and temperature, evaluate the weather conditions, if the runway is wet, if it is raining, snowing, etc. to make sure the takeoff is allowed, and it is totally safe.

We also have to deal with administrative paperwork. At some point during the preflight preparations we will be asked when it is okay for you to board the aircraft. Before you do that, your cabin attendants have been checking the passenger cabin, making sure drinks and meals, when applicable, are safely loaded in the aircraft, verifying that all emergency equipment is readily available, and that other cabin systems are in good working condition. Ground crews, normally before the crew gets on board, take care of cleaning and conditioning the interior of the aircraft to prepare it for the next flight.

THE PILOT'S BRIEFING

Later on in the cockpit, and as part of the preflight prepa- ration, the pilots discuss among themselves details of the flight. The captain decides if he or she will fly the aircraft or delegate this function to the first officer. It is a common and accepted practice that if there is more than one "sec- tor" or "leg," we split the physical flying of the airplane, always of course under the final decision of the captain and commensurate with the experience of the first officer. You may relax knowing that every first officer had been trained and can take over in the event of the incapacita- tion of the captain in flight and can safely land the air- craft. Any particulars regarding crew experience, meteor- ological conditions, particulars of the route and technical aspects of the flight are discussed in this preflight briefing.

We then must contact the control tower to get what is called the flight clearance. They will have the information from the airline on every flight departing and will provide authorization to fly the intended route to the destination and assign altitudes and times to assure safe separation between the aircraft.

Once all this is done, the paperwork is signed and the cabin attendants confirm that you are all in your seats. They perform a passenger count to make sure there are no missing passengers, and more importantly, that we don't have anybody onboard who is not supposed to be there. Now, finally, we are ready to go. It is not just a slogan. Flying you (and ourselves) safely to your destination is our priority.

CHECKLISTS

These are one of the best tools we have. There is a checklist for every phase of the operation, from preflight preparations until after shutting down the engines at the gate after the flight. For some important limitations and urgent actions to accomplish in case of some serious emergencies, there are actions that we should memorize. For everything else, we have to use checklists for our normal and most abnormal non-urgent procedures. It's not a choice, it's mandatory. This ensures that all the important items to be covered in the preflight preparation, before moving the aircraft, before and after takeoff, before approach, and before and after landing have been performed. These checklists are read on each and every flight. In the case of abnormal situations, there is a checklist to be read on that specific case, which will ensure that all appropriate actions have been accomplished to solve, or at least control, the problem. These are used as needed in specific situations. During training in the simulator, we practice all these potential abnormal situations, and of course, use all the checklists for normal and non-normal procedures as we would do in a real flight.

CHAPTER FOUR

DELAYS
MOST LIKELY CAUSES OF DELAY
AT THE GATE BEFORE DEPARTURE

Most of the time flights leave at the scheduled time. However, on some occasions, you as passengers are seated there, see the schedule time of departure come and go, and the aircraft doors are still open, or you hear the announcement from the cabin attendants that all doors have been closed, hear and see the cabin attendants (or video) safety demonstration, and the aircraft is still at the gate.

The most common causes are: weather, air traffic control, final cockpit preparations by the pilots, last-minute passengers, connecting passengers, or technical. In these situations, normally we will communicate with you through the passenger address system as soon as we can and inform you of the delay and the reason.

DELAY OR CANCELLATIONS DUE TO WEATHER

In severe weather, be it a thunderstorm, a snow storm, or something like a dense fog that is not considered severe weather but may reduce the visibility to near zero or zero, airports temporarily may close operations for safety reasons. When an airport is closed, obviously no aircraft can takeoff or land at that airfield. Very powerful winds can also cause airport closures. All of these situations will invariably cause a delay, and in extreme cases, cancellations of flights. Those cancellations may affect a few flights or hundreds or even thousands of them depending on the severity and duration of the adverse weather situation. In these cases, airlines are not normally liable since it is something totally beyond their control. However, most of them will do their best to help and accommodate the needs of the passengers. Be aware, though, that you have no right to make demands. Everybody is being affected the same as you, and as the situation improves, the airlines will do their best to get you on your way as soon as possible.

At the time of writing this book, a severe cold weather hit the United States, leading to severe delays and the cancellation of thousands of flights. I had the opportunity to read some comments and posts on the Internet. Most people seem to understand the situation; yet a few others were complaining about the irresponsibility of the airlines for cancelling the flights. Keep in mind that airlines make money when airplanes fly. Keeping aircraft on the ground leads to loss of revenue and extra expenses for an airline. That on top of the logistics of reassigning flight crews, dealing with stranded passengers, and making ground staff work overtime to deal with the situation adds to the inconvenience and extra expenses to an airline. Believe me, it's a nightmare for the airlines, too, not only for the passengers. Be assured that if an airline is cancelling multiple flights due to inclement weather, it's the right and safest thing to do.

Please refer to the section in this book related to winter operations, and you will have a better understanding of why airlines may be forced to delay or cancel flights when an airport or several airports are affected by extreme weather conditions.

DELAY DUE TO AIR TRAFFIC CONTROL

Sometimes your flight will be departing from or flying to a very busy airport or to a busy airspace. For the safety of every flight, air traffic control must establish a minimum separation on the flights. If ten flights are scheduled to depart at the same time, air traffic control establishes priorities based on certain criteria applicable to the situation. In the case of a congested airport for departure and arrivals, slot times are assigned to every flight. Sometimes this slot may be ten minutes or more from the time the flight is ready. Some other times, a slot time is assigned but the aircraft misses it for different reasons, like final checks, late passengers boarding at the last minute, etc. In this case, a new slot must be re-assigned, which means the flight will go to the bottom of the waiting line, leading to a delay.

In the case of arrival to a busy airport, the departure facility and the arrival facility must coordinate the departure of the aircraft so it arrives to the busy destination airport within a certain time frame, again to ensure the necessary separation among arriving aircraft. It may cause a delay in the departure time from the gate, even though the aircraft is ready to go. In the case of flying through congested airspaces en-route, something similar applies. The aircraft can be allowed in a certain airspace at a certain time in coordination with the air traffic control facilities, taking into consideration all the flights expected in that particular airspace. Air traffic is intense in certain areas these days, and even with all the possible altitudes available, safe separation between aircraft has to be ensured, and clear guidelines and minimums exist that must be applied by air traffic control.

Something most passengers don't know is that an aircraft cannot necessarily fly at any altitude. Even though an aircraft may be designed and certified to fly to a certain maximum altitude, which ranges between 30,000 and 45,000 feet for most commercial airliners, the higher altitudes can only be reached when the airplane is light on weight. When an airplane is loaded to its "maximum certified takeoff weight" (see definitions), it cannot reach the maximum certified altitude for that particular airplane. This is the case in most "long-haul" flights. The longer the flight, the more fuel is needed, which adds to the weight, and the more passengers it has, means more baggage as well and more weight. This means that even though a higher altitude may be available in a congested airspace, the aircraft is unable to climb to reach it. What could happen if the pilot tries to force the aircraft higher than what the weight allows? Refer to the "Questions and Answers" section in this book for the answer to that and some other common questions.

This leads to another point I want you to know about. Every aircraft at a certain weight has an optimum altitude to fly where it is the most fuel-efficient. If a commercial aircraft is forced to fly above or way below its optimum altitude, the fuel burn normally increases. Due to weight limitations and safety, the aircraft cannot climb much higher than the optimum altitude, but technically it can fly many thousands of feet below its optimum altitude. The problem is that the more distant from its optimum altitude, the more fuel it will burn. This obviously increases fuel cost for an airline, but the safety issue is the most important here, especially in long-haul flights. For every flight, the fuel consumption for the route is calculated based on flying at or near the optimum altitude. If an aircraft is forced to fly at a way lower altitude than the optimum, the fuel consumption may increase to an unacceptable level. Therefore, sometimes we choose to wait longer at the gate to ensure we will be accommodated in the airspace at or near the optimum altitude for the flight, to ensure we do not burn more fuel than we need to. We want to have the most possible fuel when we reach our destination in case there is any situation that may keep us in the air longer than expected. And remember that there is a provision in every commercial flight for extra fuel in case the flight has to be diverted to the planned alternate airport. This is fuel we always want to protect.

DELAY DUE TO FINAL COCKPIT PREPARATIONS

In most cases we finish our preparations on time. However, sometimes we encounter last minute changes that require a revision from our part. A wind direction change, a runway change, it was not raining or snowing and now it is, the airport authorities needed to close the runway we were planning to use situations like these require that we perform new calculations to ensure the optimum performance of the aircraft. An aircraft, and especially a commercial aircraft as you can imagine, is not like a car where you sit, start the engine, and there you go. Every commercial flight requires careful planning, preparation, and particular calculations for its current weight after being loaded, and the expected situations to be found during takeoff, the flight itself, and the landing. If some of these factors change at the last minute, careful revision and recalculations are required in most cases. This in turn may cause a delay. Just bear with us and keep in mind this is for your safety.

DELAYS DUE TO LAST MINUTE PASSENGERS

The airlines have a closed count of how many passengers have checked in at the counter. All those passengers are expected to board the aircraft. If somebody checks in at the counter and then does not show up at the boarding gate, this is a cause for investigation. Normally these passengers are just plainly distracted, stuck in an immigration or security line, lost in the terminal, or at the wrong gate. They are normally called through the microphones at the terminal trying to direct them to the correct gate. Once all efforts have been exhausted, if the passenger or passengers do not show up, due to safety measures, their checked baggage has to be offloaded from the aircraft, which of course takes time.

DELAYS DUE TO CONNECTING PASSENGERS

When we refer to connecting passengers, in many instances, airline schedules are built in a way that allows passengers to make connections. Normally when a passenger books a flight, either at the airline counter, with a travel agency or directly through the internet, he or she, depending on the flight, is offered several options, including approved connections through the airline schedule. Of course, delays happen for several reasons as discussed. If a flight with connecting passengers is arriving a little behind schedule, and there are no other flights available, airlines sometimes choose to delay a departing flight to wait for those connecting passengers. It is the airline's choice to delay or not a flight to wait for connecting passengers. When they do, it is normally for less than an hour. If, for example, there is a domestic flight connecting with an international departure, the airlines try their best to help those passengers make the connection within reasonable limits. I am sure that if it was your case, you would appreciate being extended this courtesy.

As explained, it normally makes economic sense for the airlines when they do it. They try hard not to disrupt the travel plans of the passengers on time at the airport. If it is 30 or 40 passengers connecting, they may delay the flight to wait for them for a few minutes up to an hour or two tops. But if it is only three or four connecting passengers, the airline may choose to absorb the cost of putting them in a later or future flight and pay for their hotel and meals if necessary.

DELAY DUE TO TECHNICAL REASONS

By far this is the least common, but still happens. Maintenance checked everything, we tested and prepared all the aircraft systems, and when we start configuring the cockpit for departure, we notice that something is not working the way it should. In these cases we must delay the flight and let maintenance take care of the problem before we depart. Rest assured that we will not take your flight into the air until we are satisfied it is one hundred percent safe, even if it means delaying it.

DELAY DUE TO THE NEED TO DE-ICE AND/OR ANTI-ICE THE AIRCRAFT

During winter operations, the aircraft needs to be treated to remove and prevent any snow or ice accumulation in its frame and engines. There is a chapter devoted to things you should know when flying in winter. Possible delays are just one of them. Please refer to that chapter for more details.

DELAYS BETWEEN THE TARMAC AND THE TAKEOFF

It is entirely possible to receive updated information on restrictions for departures at the current airport and/or arrivals at the destination airport that may require some waiting time just before takeoff. Some airports have designated areas for waiting that may be close to the runway or at a special designated area. Once again, I am sure your captain will update you as a passenger if any of these situations arise and will let you know the approximate waiting time.

CHAPTER FIVE

FACTS AND INFORMATION
THE AIR WILL NORMALLY STOP FLOWING TO THE
CABIN WHEN THE AIRCRAFT IS READY TO START THE
ENGINES. UNDERSTANDING WHY!

As you probably know, in order to start a car, a device called a starter is necessary to initially make the engine turn. The starter in the car is normally electric. On commercial jet airliners, there is also a starter, but it needs air under pressure to rotate the big engine to commence the start process. This air under pressure may be provided from an external source, but the majority of the time it is provided by the "auxiliary power unit or APU," which is the ground auxiliary unit installed in the aircraft to provide air conditioning and electricity to the aircraft on the ground (See the definitions section). Therefore, when the pilots are ready to start the engines, the air is removed from the air conditioning system and directed toward the engines, normally one at a time in order to start them. At this moment, the air stops flowing to the cabin and instinctively, many passengers reach to the air outlets on top of them trying to verify if it is open or not and checking why there is no airflow. There is nothing you can do to get air, even though the outlet is fully open. Just be patient until the engines are started. Once they are running, they will be the ones providing air for the air conditioning system, and everything will be back to normal; you will feel the air flowing again. Now you know better, and this book is meeting its purpose once more.

ABOUT THE SAFETY DEMONSTRATION

I know many of you are frequent flyers and have heard this demonstration dozens of times. Good for you, and we all trust that you by now know exactly what to do and what not to do in the event of an emergency. Being that aviation is the safest mode of transportation by far, emergencies rarely happen. However, it is well documented that during the emergencies, once in a while it still happens, that many passengers have no clue on what to do, simply because they chose to ignore the safety demonstration. This presentation is done by regulation and is in place for your protection. Unless you completely know exactly what to do regarding what is informed on this demonstration, I strongly encourage you to take the few minutes it takes to watch it and make sure you understand it. It is done for a reason. That is one of the few things we ask from you in a flight and the few things we expect from you as a passenger, just for your own safety and the safety of your fellow passengers. Every passenger who selfishly chooses to ignore the safety measures is endangering not only him or herself, but also the rest of the people onboard unnecessarily. Please keep it in mind and help us to keep you and your fellow passengers safe. Remember that even if you fly frequently and unless you only fly in one of the airlines that have a single model of aircraft, most airlines have different models of aircraft—the location of life vest, emergency exits, and other information may vary.

FROM THE TIME THE AIRCRAFT MOVES FROM THE GATE UNTIL AFTER TAKEOFF, KEEP THE FOLLOWING RECOMMENDATIONS IN MIND, EVEN BETTER, FOLLOW THEM FOR YOUR OWN SAFETY—I AM MORE THAN HAPPY TO GIVE YOU REASONS WHY

Keep your tray table stowed and your seat on the upright

position. Why? If you recline your seat on the ground, you will obstruct the exit path of the passenger seated behind you in case of an emergency evacuation. The tray table will obstruct the exit path of passengers seated in your same row or worse, hurt you in the case of a sudden stop in the runway. So even if you are seated in a window seat, make sure your tray table is securely stowed for takeoff and landing.

Keep wearing your shoes until airborne. It is common, especially for first class passengers or during long flights to see passengers remove their shoes as soon as they settle in their seats. Yes, I have flown as a passenger in economy, business, and first class, and I have seen it. Even more inviting to remove their shoes is the fact that on long-haul flights, passengers receive a travel kit containing slippers among other things. Some airlines provide these kits on the ground before departure. Many passengers immediately remove their shoes and put on the slippers. As comfortable as it may be, I strongly suggest that you wait until the aircraft is in the air. Again, if an evacuation becomes necessary before takeoff, your shoes may be in the way, you may lose time, and obstruct others while trying to retrieve and put your shoes back on, and finally, you will definitely be better of wearing your shoes in an evacuation following an incident on the tarmac or after a rejected takeoff. The same applies in the unlikely event of a crash landing. You don't know on what kind of ground you will be running, so please, keep your shoes on until after takeoff and wear them before landing. The only exception is if a water landing is necessary, and you will be boarding a life raft, especially ladies with high heel shoes. It is very unlikely that you will be involved in any of these situations, but why take a chance of making it worse?

Again, pay attention to the safety demonstration. Why? Having to do any of what is shown in the demonstration is rarely needed, as aviation keeps getting safer and safer, but there have been instances during which a passenger did not know what to do when required because he or she simply decided that paying attention to the safety demonstration was a waste of time. It is not. It is done or shown on video for a reason, and it is for you. We already have been trained on what to do. Unless you are a frequent flyer who has seen it many times for the same type of aircraft, please get familiar with that information and with the safety information card normally in the pocket of the seat in front of you or in the wall if you are in the first row. Even frequent flyers fly different types of aircraft and need to know where to locate a life vest or recognize the nearest exit. Help yourself and your cabin attendants in the event that this information becomes necessary. It may save your life.

Make sure there is nothing in the way in case of an emergency evacuation. That is the reason why everything must be either in the overhead bins or under the seat in front of you.

Make sure your seatbelt is fastened rather tight than loose, but not so tight as to completely immobilize or hurt you. It will keep you well in your seat in case of unexpected turbulence or a sudden stop during takeoff or after landing.

Make sure that you have located the closest exit as explained during the safety demonstration.

Turn off your electronic devices if instructed by your cabin attendants, especially important for takeoff and landing. Why? They may indeed interfere with essential systems in the cockpit. Rules may be a little different or have changed by the time you read this, but as I said, if the airline or the cabin attendant requests that they be turned off, please comply. See the Questions and Answers section for a more extensive explanation on this.

RECOMMENDATIONS WHILE AIRBORNE

This is normally the longest part of your journey. However, this is the part when you can relax and enjoy the flight as much as possible and one of the shortest sections in this book. Most pilots will remind you to keep your seatbelt fastened while in your seats, since as already discussed, clear-air turbulence is a fact and may happen. If it is daytime and the visibility is good, your pilot may point out some points of interest along the route. In the most recent models of aircraft, one or several map views may be available on the entertainment system, so passengers can follow the progress of the flight and the area being over flown.

Positively, keep your seatbelt fastened and stay in your seat while the seatbelt sign is illuminated. We know better, and when it is illuminated, it is because we suspect or expect that the ride may become rough. If it has been a while, the ride has been smooth, you need to get up and the seatbelt sign is still illuminated, kindly ask your cabin attendant. She may just go and check with the pilots and let you know of the reason and if it is okay for you to get up. If you happen to be enjoying a first class bed-type seat, make sure you fasten your seatbelt before you fall asleep. In this case, fasten it a little loose so you can move.

It is also highly recommended on long flights to get up and stretch your legs for a few minutes, at least every two hours. Many in-flight magazines have a page with recommended exercises while in your seat to keep the blood flowing. Sit back, relax, and enjoy the ride. Luckily with so many allowed electronic devices and improved on-board entertainment systems, now it is easier to stay busy during your flight and feel that the time goes by faster.

ARRIVAL PREPARATIONS

Cabin attendants make sure there is nothing in the way, pick up the last items the passengers may want to discard, and secure the cabin for landing. That means making sure you comply with the safety regulations regarding the back of your seat, your tray table, no items in the way, and electronics not allowed during landing turned off. In the mean time, the pilots are getting busy to prepare for the arrival and landing.

DURING DESCENT

Most airlines require that the pilots turn on the seatbelt right before starting descent or in the earlier stages of it. Air traffic control may require that the descent be interrupted momentarily to separate your aircraft from another or several turns may be required. You are better off in your seat with the seatbelt fastened. Also, this is the time when the cabin attendants start to prepare the cabin for arrival, pick up any items you may want to discard, like used cups, napkins, and glasses, and make sure everything is secured for landing.

Once again, it is important to close your tray table, put your seatback in the upright position, stow everything, wear your shoes, and turn off your electronic devices as instructed for the same reasons previously outlined.

Now with preparing for the landing, comes a common question that I prefer to address here instead of in the Questions and Answers section.

WHY ARE SOME LANDINGS SMOOTH AND SOME OTHERS NOT SO NICE?

Different reasons include:
Some pilots have a better touch than others, same as car and bus drivers. Although the landing technique is based on the same principles, there is also the personal touch within allowed parameters. Every pilot may have a different feeling when it comes to the landing maneuver. Having said that, we all have had bad landings, excellent landings, and everything in between. Like on everything,

some pilots have better records than others. Experience also plays a role. You can expect better landings from a captain or first officer who has been flying a particular model for long time than from a pilot relatively new to the model. We captains normally share the landings with the first officers to help them gain more experience. Something we discuss in our briefing, if we do not know each other very well, is our mutual experience. We particularly want to know how experienced is a first officer, and then we decide to let him or her do the landing in an airport in generally easier conditions, like little or no wind and good visibility, leaving for ourselves the most challenging operations. Like in any career, as new surgeons must perform their first operations to gain experience, new pilots must do their first landings to gain experience as well. But as mentioned before, no pilot is allowed in the cockpit of an airliner until he or she has demonstrated to be completely ready and passed all the rigorous trainings programs that airlines have in place.

Meteorological conditions also may affect the quality of the landing. If there is bad weather or even in good weather, high intensity winds exist, and we have to concentrate harder, and in these cases, for safety reasons, we want to bring the airplane to the ground as soon as possible. If the runway is contaminated with water or snow, a firm landing is the way to go to ensure the wheels make good contact with the runway and the brakes work more efficiently under such degraded conditions. We also need more runway distance to stop the aircraft, so we don't want to waste it by delaying the landing and trying to make it smooth. In these situations, sometimes it is nice, some others not so nice, but be comforted that it is the safest course of action. The same principle applies for short runways. No point in making a smooth landing and then running out of the end of the runway. Of course, we do not blindly go and land in the runway, short or long. Depending on the weight of the aircraft, the wind direction, and the condition of the runway, meaning if it is dry, wet, or contaminated with snow or ice, we must perform calculations and consult tables to verify it is safe to land on that particular runway, at that particular aircraft weight, and under the current airport conditions.

THE "GO-AROUND" MANEUVER AND ITS REASONS

A go-around or missed approach is simply interrupting the approach or the landing. It can be commenced at certain altitudes during final approach and even upon touching the runway. You will feel how the aircraft accelerates and climbs again away from the runway. It is natural for most passengers to feel apprehensive and nervous thinking something is wrong. Not so. I will mention several reasons that may trigger this situation, but the common denominator is that it is the safest course of action, and after the initial surprise, you should try to relax and tell yourself it was the best thing to happen at that moment. After all, the aircraft is safely flying as it was moments ago, before it had to climb again.

The go-around may be the pilot's judgment and decision or mandated by the air traffic controller. An air traffic controller may order an aircraft to discontinue the landing maneuver due to being too close to another aircraft that is about to land or due to another aircraft or a vehicle occupying the runway for the intended landing. I am sure you will agree with avoiding a ground collision on the runway.

A pilot may initiate a go-around on his own for some other reasons:

He or she feels the approach is unstable, meaning the altitude or the speed is excessive for a safe landing and stopping on the runway, in which case it's better to climb back and do it again safely.

The visibility may be reduced. Every airport has published approach procedures and the minimum altitude at which the pilot may descend safely until establishing visual contact with the runway and completing a safe landing. If upon reaching that altitude, the pilots don't see the runway, it is mandatory to do a go-around. If in the captain's opinion, it is safe to try another approach, he or she will do so. This entitles communication with the air traffic controllers to see if conditions are expected to improve and the fuel on board is sufficient to perform a "holding" while waiting for conditions to improve.

There may be dangerous winds and the pilot does not feel comfortable landing the aircraft under such conditions. The same situation as the previous paragraph applies.

In most cases, once the pilot has taken care of priority tasks, he or she will communicate with the passengers to explain the situation and notify the passengers of the next course of action and what to expect.

There are published procedures for every runway, so your pilots know exactly in what direction to fly and to what altitude to climb after a go-around. In all cases the air traffic controllers will be informed, and they may instruct the pilot to follow the published missed approach procedure or will issue specific instructions for the pilots to follow.

HOW, IN LAYMAN'S TERMS, CAN PILOTS FLY, DESCEND, AND FIND THEIR WAY TO AN AIRPORT AT NIGHT OR WHEN THERE IS NO VISIBILITY?

One of the questions I get the most from people not versed in aviation matters has to do with how pilots find the runway to land in poor visibility conditions or in the dark. As I have been doing throughout this book, I don't want to get too technical, but I will gladly try to explain in easy to understand language.

In the very old days, before the jet age, pilots did not have the array of facilities we enjoy today. Therefore landing in poor visibility was simply not an option. As technology evolved, ground facilities to help pilots became more and more sophisticated. Nowadays, those facilities, coupled with onboard equipment and the latest generation aircraft, and I mean aircraft made from the 1980s and forward, are capable of descending to low altitudes approaching the runway in poor visibility and even land automatically. Still, pilot intervention in adjusting some settings in the cockpit is required. I will expand on that later.

INSTRUMENT LANDING SYSTEMS

Modern aircraft and airports are equipped with instruments and systems that allow an aircraft to descend and land at an airport in near-zero visibility. Special training is required for the crew, and all equipment on board and on the ground must be fully functional. There are different warnings in the cockpit to alert the crew if any of this equipment lacks the integrity to perform what is called a low visibility approach. Of course, if extreme weather conditions cause an airport closure, attempting any kind of approach is not allowed. These kind of approaches are normally flown with the autopilot in charge of flying the aircraft, and the pilots simply monitor the operation, ready to take over and perform a go-around in case anything goes wrong. But the last is a rare occurrence, not the rule, and rarely happens. However, crews trained to carry on these types of approaches, as part of their training, are always prepared for any undesired event and practice them extensively in the flight simulator.

Every major airport and most regional airports have one or more radio facilities installed that can be tuned by navigational radios on the aircraft. There are two types of radios in the aircraft: communication radios and navigation radios. The navigation radios are the ones that interest us in this explanation. Depending on the facilities installed on the airport, these radios receive signals that tell the pilots where the airport is located and the exact position of the aircraft. Every airport has a minimum altitude based on the facilities installed at which the aircraft may descend without visibility based on that particular facility and the capability of the onboard equipment to receive the signals from that or those facilities.

The most sophisticated system is called exactly as the titled of this section, "Instrument Landing System," or ILS as we in the aviation world call it. Most airports where airlines operate have this system installed, and we normally use it, even in good visibility conditions. Of course, we need to know how to land the airplane visually if this equipment fails, provided we have established visual contact with the runway. Airline pilots are supposed to be trained for that.

In order to conduct low visibility approaches, the equipment and radio facilities on the ground and the appropriate equipment on the aircraft must be fully operational. The ILS sends two signals to the aircraft. One aligns the aircraft perfectly with the runway, and the second shows exactly the vertical trajectory or glide path that the aircraft must follow to reach the runway at the exact point. By following these signals, either using the autopilot or flying the aircraft manually, we can find the runway in low visibility. However, manually flying these approaches is restricted in most cases to a minimum altitude of 200 feet or sixty meters, which is already pretty low. If there is no visual reference with the runway at that point, a go-around must be accomplished.

Before every approach, we get the information on the expected conditions of the airport and the runway or runways in use, normally through a dedicated radio frequency, through the air traffic controller, or in latest generation aircraft through electronic radio equipment that will display the information on a screen and will allow us to print it on board aircraft equipped with a printer, as most latest generation aircraft are. In any case, we have the means to get the information. That way we know if the airport has poor visibility, the intensity and direction of the wind, and the runway or runways in use.

Now, since about thirty years ago to the present, the advance on technology allows approaches in almost zero visibility. However, there are more rigorous requirements. The airport, the aircraft, and the crew must be approved and certified to conduct this type of approach. Even though an airport may have the facilities to conduct this type of approach, the aircraft may not have the required equipment or even if the aircraft has the equipment, the airline or the crew may not be approved or certified to conduct these types of approaches because they have not undergone the necessary extra training. Most major airlines worldwide, however, are approved to conduct these types of approaches; although not all aircraft on their fleets may have the capabilities to do so, or some of their newest pilots may have not received the appropriate training to do so yet.

These are just facts that will affect if your flight crew will be conducting an approach in very low visibility. However, every airline pilot is trained to descend using an instrument landing system as low as 200 feet with horizontal visibility of at least 550 meters. As stated before, if the crew decides to interrupt the approach and climb again, you should not be alarmed but relieved that your crew is taking the safest course of action for that given circumstance.

Going back to the basic requirements to conduct a low visibility approach below sixty meters (or 200 feet) is that the autopilot must fly the aircraft, and the pilots become the monitors of the system always prepared to take over and interrupt the approach climbing back to safety if the system should malfunction. The pilot's hands should be guarding the controls at all times, prepared for that unlikely possibility of a malfunction; nothing is left to chance. However, as I mentioned before, pilot intervention is still necessary for example to set the aircraft speed, to extend the flaps and reduce the speed accordingly to the landing speed, and to lower the landing gear or put down the wheels for landing (in layman's terms). None of this is automatic, although, in most cases, the thrust levers or aircraft throttles—one per engine—have an automatic function that will adjust the speed to that selected by the pilot. But we must help the autopilot by doing all those other things. The autopilot, with the correct information received from the pilot, does a beautiful job flying the aircraft to the runway, landing it smoothly, and keeping it on the center until the speed is reduced to the minimum to abandon the runway. I must mention that most modern aircraft have automatic brakes, too, with different settings to be selected by the pilot according to the conditions. So the landing maneuver, the extension of the spoilers, or the speedbrakes upon touchdown, and the braking are fully automatic, and the pilots become the backup in this case. Only "thrust reversers" have to be manually activated by the pilot after landing.

And talking about the thrust reversers, they are nothing else than a system that redirects the air to the front of the engines instead of the back to assist in slowing down the aircraft. That is the engine accelerating noise that you hear in most cases after landing, the pilot activating the reversers and accelerating the engines to assist in stopping the aircraft. Nowadays there are noise restrictions in place at several airports near heavily populated areas, at night or both, where pilots are forbidden to activate the reversers at high power unless there is an emergency. Just for your information and peace of mind, the engine reversers are not taken into account to calculate the required distance to stop an airplane after landing or on the rare occasions when a takeoff needs to be rejected or aborted. Therefore these restrictions have no negative effects whatsoever in safely stopping the aircraft or in other words, safety is not affected at all if they are not used. They are part of the engine system and are like a bonus, just to make the brakes work less after landing, but they are technically not required to stop the aircraft. That is why sometimes you hear them after landing and some other times you don't.

Once the airplane reduces its speed enough to vacate the runway, the pilot—at the touch of a switch—disconnects all the automatic system and takes over to "taxi" the airplane out of the runway and to the gate. In extremely low visibility conditions, depending on the airport ground equipment and lighting system, there may also be a vehicle with a big sign showing FOLLOW ME, waiting for the aircraft to guide it to the appropriate gate or parking position.

Now you have an understanding on how we manage to find the runway when you cannot see anything but clouds, rain, snow, or a dark night out your window.

CHAPTER SIX

WARNING SYSTEMS

To add to your peace of mind, I would like to let you know that one of the most important systems on an aircraft is the warning system. We have warnings for every conceivable unsafe situation in the aircraft. If we have done our job correctly, we should not normally hear these warnings. But we are only human, humans may be distracted, forget things, or just have one of those days, and with that in mind, the warning system is an integral part of an airplane as an added safety feature and a great backup for pilots. We even have a form of warning on the ground before we accept the aircraft to tell us if any of the warning systems are not working properly. This system, as all the others, is periodically revised and tested by maintenance.

Many pilots retest them during preflight as part of the preflight preparation. You may have heard some of the voice warnings as you enter the aircraft or if you sit in the forward part of the aircraft during boarding. It means the pilot is retesting the system.

There are aural warnings, either by voice, alarm bell, siren or tones, message warnings on a screen, and light warnings. The most serious warnings provide all three: lights, messages, and aural to ensure attention.

Instrument failures also provide visual warnings in the form of an internal flag that shows on the instrument or a warning message in computerized instruments. Older airplanes without computerized screens do not have message warnings, but still aural and lights, as well as flags.

An internal flag will show in an instrument covering it partially to tell the pilot that the instrument is not working properly. When the flag is not in view, the instrument is reliable and working correctly.

To satisfy your curiosity, I will name as many as I can remember per phase of flight.

During pre-flight and on the ground:
- As I said before, there is a message and light warning if any of the warning systems are not working properly.
- If a door is not properly closed
- If the fuel is insufficient for the planned flight as entered in the flight computers
- If there is a fire on the APU, one of the engines, or in a cargo compartment

Before takeoff:
- If the flaps are not extended in the proper position for takeoff
- If the adjustable tail surface is not within its takeoff range position
- If the parking brake is not released
- If the surfaces over the wings (speedbrakes or spoilers) are not flushed with the wing, meaning completely in their stowed position.

During takeoff roll and in flight:
- If there is a loss of thrust in one of the engines
- If there is a fire in one of the engines, in a cargo compartment, or in the area where the landing gear is stowed during flight
- If there is a loss of pressurization
- If any of the doors unlock, although this is normally detected at the gate before even the airplane moves. In flight, the pressurization normally keeps the doors locked on top of their own locks and levers.
- If there is a problem with any of the electrical generators or in the electrical system of the aircraft
- If there is a problem with any of the hydraulic systems. Airliners have at least 3 of them.
- If another aircraft gets too close. See "TCAS"

- If there is a change in altitude not programmed or executed by the pilots
- If the speed is too low or too fast
- Generally speaking, every malfunction will generate some type of warning.

During descent and approach:
- On top of all the mentioned during flight, there are some warnings particularly related to the approach to land.
- If the aircraft gets too close to terrain away from the airport. Latest generation airliners from the past twenty years include a database of all terrain worldwide or are tailored to their area of operation, which shows on a screen where and how high the terrain is in the area the aircraft is flying. A loud aural warning, "TERRAIN, TERRAIN, PULL UP, PULL UP" will be heard in the cockpit. Unless there is positive visual verification that terrain is not a threat, the mandatory reaction for us pilots is to apply maximum thrust to the engines and climb away until the warning ceases and only then investigate the cause.
- If the aircraft descends below a certain altitude with the wheels up, a loud aural warning will be heard as "TOO LOW, GEAR." The entire structure containing the wheels is called landing gear.
- If the flaps are not in a landing position below a certain altitude during final descent, a loud aural warning as "TOO LOW, FLAPS" will be heard in the cockpit.
- If the aircraft deviates from the programmed glide path to the runway the aural warning "GLIDE SLOPE" is heard in the cockpit.
- If at low altitude before landing or during the takeoff there is a rapid change in wind velocity or direction known as "windshear," since it may have an adverse effect on aircraft controllability. The aural warning heard will be "WINDSHEAR AHEAD" if the radar detects it ahead of time or just "WINDSHEAR" if it is

suddenly experienced. There is a specific reaction and maneuver that we are trained for in this situation.

All these warnings have established procedures that we airline pilots must follow regardless of the airline. They are, of course, very similar and beyond the scope of this book. Suffice to know that they all are designed and established to return the aircraft to a safe altitude where the cause for the warning can be investigated. In most cases, except when there is no doubt about the safe position of the aircraft, or when there is sufficient time to correct the situations, they are another cause for a go-around, which is normally the safest course of action. As discussed, the go-around will bring the aircraft back up to a safe altitude where another approach and landing can be attempted after assessing the situation.

CHAPTER SEVEN

THINGS TO BE AWARE OF WHEN FLYING DURING WINTER

First of all, be aware that in heavy winter storms, affected airports may probably be closed for hours until the storm passes and then for the time necessary to clean runways and "taxiways" of accumulated snow.

Snow and rain in freezing temperatures adheres to all parts of the aircraft. It creates several problems:

All that ice accumulation increases the weight of the aircraft, and that is a weight that is not accounted for. As explained in another part of this book, the weight of the aircraft is limited by several factors. When calculating the maximum weight at which the aircraft can takeoff, this extra weight due to ice accumulation will invalidate all the calculations. Therefore it must be removed.

If ice accumulates in the cavities and spaces necessary for the movable surfaces of the aircraft, it may block the movement of these surfaces that are essential to control the aircraft.

Ice accumulated in external aircraft sensors may create erroneous readings in important flight instruments. It must be completely removed from these areas and prevented to form again.

Ice accumulated in the front part of the wing will alter the wing design necessary to allow the airplane to fly. Hence the wings must be totally free of ice.

Ice or snow in any part of the aircraft would blow during takeoff and may be ingested by the engines causing the engines to lose power, flame out, or fail completely. This is particularly true in aircraft with rear-mounted engines. Yet another reason to make sure the aircraft is free of ice, snow, or any other contaminant.

The process of de-icing and anti-icing the aircraft takes some time and obviously in most cases will cause a delay. With outside temperatures as high as ten degrees Celsius (fifty degrees Fahrenheit) or below, consideration must be given to de-ice the aircraft if humidity is present. Remember that an aircraft that has just arrived has been flying at high altitudes. At the normal altitudes at which airliners fly, the temperature is very low. As you probably know, the higher you climb at the altitudes at which airplanes normally fly, the cooler the outside temperature is. If you live or have visited a city located at a high altitude above sea level, you have realized it is colder. You will experience the same temperature decrease as you climb a mountain. Airliners normally fly at altitudes between 29,000 and 41,000 feet. The temperatures at those altitudes, even in summertime, are below minus thirty to minus sixty degrees Celsius. Of course, the air conditioning system on board maintains a comfortable temperature. The temperature of the fuel contained in the tanks, however, decreases as well during flights at these high altitudes. Fuel is contained in tanks inside the wings and in the center "fuselage." For your relief, here is another piece of information. The freezing point of jet fuel is minus forty degrees Celsius (minus forty degrees Fahrenheit), way below the freezing point of water. After a long flight, the fuel temperature may be well below zero. That will make the wings very cold. The problem resides in the fact that even though the fuel will remain in liquid state because of its very low freezing point, any drop of water in contact with the wing will freeze since its freezing point, as you know, is zero degrees Celsius (thirty-two degrees Fahrenheit). High humidity or even a drizzle may create ice in the wings under these conditions, which may be undetectable to the naked eye. As part of the preflight exterior inspection of the aircraft, maintenance and/or one of the pilots feels the wings by touching them to detect possible ice buildup that may not be easily detectable by sight. In any case, when doubt exists, the aircraft will be de-iced. This is done by using approved heated liquids containing chemical ingredients for this purpose.

If no precipitation exists, there is no need to anti-ice the aircraft. The de-icing by itself will remove any possible contaminant in the form of clear ice. Of course, when there is visible snow or ice on the aircraft, de-icing will be performed.

Anti-icing is required when precipitation exists, and the temperature is below ten degrees Celsius (fifty degrees Fahrenheit). It is performed in one step, which includes both de-icing and anti-icing fluids in the same application or in two steps: de-icing first and then a second application of anti-icing fluids. While these procedures are performed, normally the airflow will be cut to the cabin to prevent excessive chemical odors. Once the operation is finished, normally the airflow will be restored within one or two minutes. You may still perceive some particular odor, but it will dissipate shortly thereafter. In most cases you will be informed beforehand when this operation is being performed. If for whatever reason your crew is busy and misses informing you, now you know what those trucks spraying your aircraft are doing and why. When it is raining or snowing during winter, this is a common sight at the airport.

I would like to add here, since it has and will continue to happen, if there is a lengthy wait after the anti-icing treatment while the aircraft goes to the takeoff runway, your aircraft may have to return to the gate or go to a predetermined spot in the airport to be anti-iced again. Why? Because these fluids have a specific time after which they start losing their effectiveness, depending on the type of fluid and the type of precipitation. Your pilots have tables to use to determine for how long they can wait until takeoff before having to reapply anti-icing fluid. So, if it ever happens to you, now you know better, and there is no cause for alarm. The inconvenience of an added delay is for your safety. Once again, I am sure that in most cases your captain will speak to you and your fellow passengers through the passenger address system and explain the situation.

Once in flight, the high speed and friction will normally prevent ice from forming on the aircraft structure. However, the engines have an anti-ice system that is used when required on the ground and in flight.

ENGINE ANTI-ICE

During winter operations, the engines also need to be protected from ice forming inside, which could cause the engine to fail if continuous and high amounts of snow, ice, or water at near-freezing temperatures enter the engine. The engines have a system that provides heated air from the same engine to heat it at the front part, since the rest of the engine inside, once running, is hot by the same combustion process. During winter, the pilots activate this anti-ice system for the engines as soon as it is running on the tarmac before taxiing the aircraft to the runway. Even during summer, when the aircraft is in flight, as the temperature decreases with altitude, if visible moisture exists, like clouds, rain or snow, the pilots will activate the engine anti-ice system to protect it during the low temperatures at high altitudes. However, if the air is clear, regardless of the low temperature, then the engine anti-ice system is not required.

HOW IS THE STRUCTURE OF THE AIRCRAFT PROTECTED FROM ICE IN FLIGHT?

Due to the heat generated by friction and to the speed of the aircraft in flight, ice does not normally form on the aircraft in flight or if it does it is in tiny quantities. Only some parts of the wings are heated in flight as needed.

Before takeoff, as explained, when icy conditions exist at the airport, the aircraft is properly treated to prevent ice from forming on the structure and affecting the aerodynamic design of the aircraft, which would be dangerous at takeoff. As the airspeed increases in flight, this anti-ice fluid will be shed off the aircraft frame.

THE WINDSHIELDS MUST ALSO BE HEATED

The pilot's windshields and lateral windows in the cockpit are also heated. There are two main reasons to heat those windows. The first is to prevent fog from forming and the second is to increase impact resistance. *Impact against what?* you may be wondering. The simple answer is birds. Birds can't fly at the higher altitudes an airliner flies. However, some of them do fly up to approximately 10,000 feet (3,000 meters). In order for an aircraft to reach those high cruise altitudes and to descend for landing, it most obviously crosses the low altitudes from the airport up to the high "flight levels" during climb and descends from those "flight levels" for landing. While at low altitudes, the risk of a bird impact always exists. Who does not remember the famous case in 2009 in New York when an aircraft shortly after takeoff hit a flock of birds and was forced to make an emergency landing in the Hudson River? Kudos here and my respects to Captain Chesley "Sully" Sullenberg for his quick thinking and such a skillfully done maneuver. Of course, the birds hit a more critical part of the aircraft, but this was a rare occurrence—you probably never heard before—that thanks to Captain Sullenberg and his training, but especially his calmness and cold blood in such a critical and stressful situation, ended happily. And you have not heard of something similar after that event. It may have happened before that a bird damaged one of the engines of an aircraft, but not more than one at the same time. It was an exceptional occurrence with a very happy ending, but the fact of the matter is that a bird impacting with the airplane or vice versa is always a possibility.

About 10,000 birds and other wildlife strikes were reported for USA civil aircraft in 2011 alone. Commercial aviation aircraft engines are designed to keep working even after ingesting a four-pound bird. However, as you may know, some species of birds weigh more than that and that is when a bird ingested by a running engine may cause that engine to fail.

Going back to the windshields, if they are not heated, and there is an impact with a bird, the possibility of it breaking increases substantially. The heat provides flexibility to resist most bird impacts. Aircraft windshields are designed to withstand air pressure at 500 "knots" (about 620 miles per hour or 950 kilometers per hour) and survive hitting a bird without catastrophic failure. Heating them normally through electrical internal heating elements is an important part to guarantee this resistance. The two most likely causes of cracked windshields are simply the internal heat system being misapplied or not heating uniformly or having a bird hit it at a really high rate of speed in the air. By regulations, in most places and with a few exceptions, aircraft have a speed limit of 250 knots (288 mph or 460 km/h) below 10,000 feet. One of the reasons is to reduce the severity of an impact with a bird at the altitudes where they may be encountered. Above 10,000 feet, airliners normally fly at speeds between 280 and 340 knots before transitioning to measuring the speed in percentage of sound speed, also called the "Mach number." For more on this, refer to the definitions section.

I must add here that most airliners' windshields are made of not one but two, and in some cases three, panes of glass at least half an inch thick, so if one breaks or cracks, in most cases the other pane remains intact and the flight normally may continue to a safe landing. It will most likely cause a diversion to land in the nearest suitable airport for safety reasons.

Knowing all we know, it is still not a comforting sight

for us pilots to fly with a cracked windshield in front of us. But even in the rare and unlikely event that the windshield would break completely, the aircraft is still able to fly. It will certainly not cause any major damage to the aircraft or affect in any way its flying capabilities. Yes, the air impact and noise entering the cockpit will be annoying, but by reducing speed to the minimum to sustain flight, it will be greatly reduced. If the visibility is affected in one of the windshields, the other pilot will make the landing.

One of the most infamous cases of cracked windshields occurred in 1990, when a windshield panel blew out on a British Airways flight, nearly sucking the pilot out the window. The plane was still able to fly, and the copilot landed the aircraft safely. The captain survived.

For your comfort, I personally don't have knowledge of any other case of an airliner windshield completely breaking in flight. I personally have had two experiences of one of the panes cracking in flight, and on both occasions, we landed safely.

Next time you are sitting in a window seat, notice that your window also has two panes, the one you can touch, and you can see there is another pane outside flushed with the fuselage. Since a lateral impact is not critical, they do not need to be heated.

CHAPTER EIGHT

UNDERSTANDING THE EXTERIOR LIGHTS
OF AN AIRCRAFT

Since you may be curious about the colored lights on the aircraft, and I have been asked about them, I decided to include information on the topic as well. If you could not care less, just skip this part.

The left wing tip or end of the wing on every airplane has a red light in the forward or middle position and a white light at the rear end of the wing tip. The right wing tip has a green light in the forward or middle area and a white light at the rear end. This color code helps ground air traffic controllers at night to identify the direction in which an aircraft is moving. The relative direction of an aircraft sighted in flight, can also be determined by looking at this red or green light. Basically, the red light means you are looking at the left wing of the aircraft, and it is either stationary on the ground or moving from right to left of the observer's eye. It can also be moving on a parallel track in the same direction if it is to your right or in the opposite direction if it is to your left.

The opposite is true. Sighting a green light means that you are looking at the right wing of the aircraft. On the ground, a green light on the aircraft means it may be stopped or moving in a parallel track if it is to your left or in the opposite direction if it is to your right.

The white lights at the rear of the wing and at the very end of the tail are used to identify the aircraft position, and they are particularly useful at night in ground operations and in making the aircraft more conspicuous in flight. It helps us identify another aircraft at night that is moving right ahead of us in the same taxiway.

There are the beacon lights. These lights, red in color,

are located one on top and one at the bottom of the fuselage and blink all the time when activated. These lights are on every time the aircraft is moving, even while being towed with the engines off and always before starting the first engine until turning the last engine off at the parking gate or in the parking position. The only time these lights are off is when the aircraft is parked with its engines shut down.

The rest of the lights to be described are white lights. There are flasher lights in the wing tips as well. These are turned on when the aircraft is taking the runway for takeoff and remain activated throughout the flight until vacating the runway after landing. They are used to indicate an airplane is occupying or crossing a runway and also to make the aircraft more noticeable in flight at night. We use them day or night though. There is the logo light that illuminates the company logo in the tail of the aircraft, and it is mainly used at night.

There is also a white light in the fuselage that illuminates the wing. It is used for inspection of the wing at night and also to make the aircraft more noticeable at night or in low visibility conditions during ground operations. Most airliners have lights in the area where the wing and fuselage joins that illuminate the area forward of the aircraft similar to the lights on some cars that illuminate along with the turning signal to offer extra illumination in the direction of the turn. The most common name they receive is "turn off lights," although it may be different depending on the aircraft model. We use those when taxiing the aircraft at night to illuminate the taxiway on the ground into which we intend to turn, to provide extra illumination to the sides of the runway during takeoff and landing, and to make the aircraft more visible during flight at low altitudes for a period after takeoff and during the final descent until landing.

There is also a light or lights attached to the structure where the nose wheel is located. It is intended to be illuminated any time the aircraft is moving to alert ground personnel, ground vehicles, and other aircraft that the aircraft is about to start moving or is moving already. It will remain on for as long as the airplane is moving on the ground. Of course, at night, it also illuminates the area ahead of the aircraft, showing the pilot the taxiway or runway.

Last, but not least, are the landing lights. Some aircraft have them on the wing tips, some others in the wings, and yet others in the root area between the wings and the fuselage. Regardless of the position, they all accomplish the same function: illuminating the runway as much as possible for takeoff and for landing. Landing lights and turnoff lights remain illuminated for a period after takeoff, normally until passing 10,000 feet (about 3,000 meters of altitude)—about the elevation of the airport—when they are turned off until final descent— arriving at destination—when normally below 10,000 feet, we turn them on again to make the airplane more noticeable for approach and landing.

At high altitudes, when two aircraft cross nearby paths, it is a common practice to turn on the landing lights momentarily, mostly as a salute, and also to make their positions more noticeable to each other.

CHAPTER NINE

QUESTIONS AND ANSWERS

WHAT WOULD HAPPEN IF THE PILOT TRIES TO PUSH THE AIRCRAFT HIGHER THAN THE MAXIMUM ALTITUDE IT CAN CLIMB?

The engines will not be able to provide enough power for the aircraft to continue climbing if the aircraft is heavy. The heavier the aircraft, the lower the maximum altitude it can reach, even if using the maximum power of the engines. As a result, if the aircraft continues to climb, the speed will start decreasing. If this is not corrected, the aircraft will continue to slow down to the point that the minimum required speed to sustain flight at that altitude will be reached, and the aircraft will not be able to stay flying at that altitude. If the pilot does not keep the speed up by descending to the correct altitude, the aircraft will "stall," or in other words, the wings will no longer be able to sustain flight. If the aircraft is pushed into this situation, it will first provide a strong sound and vibrating on the controls warning the pilots. If the situation is still not corrected and the warning ignored, the aircraft will start to shake and vibrate, indicating an impending loss of lift. If there is still no reaction from the pilots, it will fall out of control. That is the reason why we perform calculations and never climb above the maximum certified altitude for the current weight. Nowadays in modern aircraft, these calculations are performed electronically and always checked by both pilots to ensure accuracy.

WHY DOES MY AIRPLANE SOMETIMES CHANGE ALTITUDE DURING FLIGHT?

There are several reasons:

To avoid or escape turbulence or rough air. Sometimes an aircraft can climb over a thunderstorm depending on its actual weight. Other times, there may be clear-air turbulence at certain altitudes. Mostly from reports from other pilots passed to air traffic control, is it possible to know at what altitudes the turbulence is less intense or nonexistent. In those cases, if the fuel consumption calculation allows, your pilot may choose to change altitude to provide you with a better ride and allow the cabin attendants to safely serve you.

In long flights, it is common to feel that the airplane climbs every two hours or so. This is done to save fuel. As explained in another part of this book, the engines may consume less fuel at higher altitudes, provided that altitude is the optimum for the current weight of the aircraft. As fuel is burned, the weight of the aircraft gradually decreases and the optimum altitude for the aircraft increases. That is the main reason why on long or mid-range flights your aircraft may be climbing progressively as it burns fuel.

To avoid conflict with another aircraft that may be flying at the same altitude. In these cases, air traffic control may instruct an aircraft to climb or descend to a different altitude to maintain proper separation with another aircraft.

WHAT EXACTLY IS CLEAR-AIR TURBULENCE AND WHY IT HAPPENS?

Clear-air turbulence, abbreviated in the aviation world as CAT, is as the name implies: turbulence or rough air that happens in the absence of any clouds in perfectly clear air.

It is caused when masses of air moving at different speeds meet. It may happen at the medium to high altitudes where commercial jets normally fly. It may be experienced near mountain ranges where the air is forced to change direction, climb, and descend in the areas nearby. Clear-air turbulence is virtually impossible to detect. Clear-air turbulence hits without warning and may be severe at times. It has caused injuries to passengers and cabin attendants in the past, forcing aircraft to make unscheduled landings. Unfortunately, due to global warming, it is expected that this condition may become more frequent. That is one of the main reasons we insist that you keep your seatbelt fasten while in your seat, even though the seatbelt sign may not be illuminated.

HOW DOES THE AIRCRAFT GET PRESSURIZED AND WHY IS THAT SO IMPORTANT?

The air provided by the air-conditioned system is retained inside the aircraft creating the pressurization. Pressurized aircraft have one, or in some cases, two valves in the fuselage that are actuated automatically according to how the pilot programs the system. In the rare event that the automatic system fails, there is a warning for that, and the pilots have a backup system to control them manually. They are, of course, normally operated in automatic mode, and the system does a beautiful job maintaining a comfortable rate of change of pressurization levels. The aircraft may be climbing or descending at 3,000 feet per minute while the cabin—thanks to the pressurization system—climbs between 300 to 500 feet per minute, maximum.

When you hear during the safety demonstration the parts that refer to a "sudden change in cabin pressure" and the "oxygen masks dropping," this happens if the pressurization cannot be maintained at safe levels. After a certain altitude, the brain and other vital organs cannot function the way they should, because the higher the altitude, the less oxygen in the air. That is why it is important to have a mask installed for every seat on the aircraft. You may have probably heard of people climbing high mountains and passing out. Now you know the reason and why it is important to keep the cabin at a safe altitude by means of the pressurization system. Your aircraft may be flying at a real altitude of 40,000 feet, but the cabin is maintained at a comfortable 7,000 feet.

Adding a note, if for whatever reason there is an opening or an explosion, the air under pressure is forced violently out, taking with it whatever is not secured. Also, since the temperature outside will be many degrees under zero, the sudden change in temperature will create a fog that will make it virtually impossible to see for several minutes. This is not meant to alarm you. I said several times that I wanted to provide some facts and information. I believe in my career, I have heard of just two such occurrences, and in both cases, the planes landed safely. The unfortunate fatality in one of them was a cabin attendant. Both cases were many years ago. The rest of it, you have probably seen in the movies.

The pressurization system is how you can be assured that if somebody tries to open a door in flight, there is no way for a human being to be able to do it.

HOW CAN I MINIMIZE THE DISCOMFORT OF THE PRESSURE CHANGES?

I am no doctor or medical expert, but I can talk based on my experience of what works for me and many of my fellow crew members. We are all humans, so I am sure some of these resources may work for you, too.

Normally the hardest part is during descent. Chewing gum, or for those of us who dislike gum, sucking on one of those cough drops or Halls® candies helps a lot during descent, since you have to frequently swallow the juice that comes out of it. That swallowing helps to open the sinuses and ear canals relieving the pressure. Conversely, eating may not be a good idea since every time you open your mouth to put food in it, you involuntarily inhale air through the mouth as well, which compounds the problem. Avoid eating during descent except to chew gum or keeping one of those juicy candies in your mouth. In those cases, you don't have to open it to put in more. Trying to yawn may do the trick as well.

Avoid, at all costs, flying if you have a cold and the subsequent congestion. During descent, that congestion may not allow to equalize the pressure in your sinuses and ear canals, and the pain is intense. You can even rupture one or both your eardrums. It is nothing short of desperation what you can experience by trying to ease the pressure to no avail and feeling how it increases more and more during descent. I know it firsthand and never want to experience it again. I landed with tears in my eyes and was grounded for five weeks. That was in my early years flying as a copilot, but I still remember it well. So if you have a cold, do yourself a favor and try not to fly.

WHY IS MY AIRCRAFT FLYING IN A CIRCLING PATTERN?

This is called "holding." There are several reasons for an aircraft to hold in order to delay its arrival:
- May be due to too many aircraft arriving at the same time, in which case air traffic controllers need to use this resource to organize and order the aircraft for arrival.
- Bad weather at the destination airport is another reason. The airport may have reduced visibility restricting the arrivals or may be closed due to a passing storm, an incident requiring momentary closure of the runway.
- The country's president arriving at that same airport or a safety-related incident in the airport requiring the

authorities to close the airport to investigate.
- The holding can also be instructed by air traffic control to increase separation with other aircraft.
- Less frequently, it is requested by the pilot to have more time to deal with a special situation that may require extra preparation or time to make a decision.

Rest assured, every flight includes fuel to perform these holdings for at least 30 minutes. When we foresee a situation like bad weather at a destination or high flow of aircraft into an airport, we add extra fuel to be able to stay in the air longer and to be able to perform a holding. Waiting for our turn to finally land at the intended destination means not having to "divert" to another airport, causing inconvenience to you and your fellow passengers and extra expenses to the airline.

Normally the place to execute these holdings is published on air navigation charts, so air traffic control can instruct us to hold at a specified published position. Since these positions are fixed and well specified, there may be other aircraft holding there as well, but at a different altitude. Therefore, don't be surprised or scared if you see other aircraft that seem too close slightly above or below your aircraft. We know they are there and each aircraft has an assigned altitude, safely separated from other aircraft that may be in the same holding pattern. We are all listening to the same air traffic controller. They have all these aircraft under radar surveillance and will bring them to lower altitudes and towards the airport commencing with the one at the lowest altitude. Once that altitude is vacated, the rest of the aircraft will be brought to lower altitudes one by one and into the airport in an orderly fashion. It is fairly common to descend in the holding pattern before proceeding to the destination airport as the aircraft below vacates a lower altitude.

Normally we will notify you of the holding, and the air traffic controller tells us for how long we can expect to hold. That way we know if we have enough fuel to do it or if we just have to fly to our safety alternate destination for which, as explained in another section, we have reserve fuel as well.

I CAN SEE THE AIRPORT RIGHT THERE. WHY IS THE PILOT FLYING AWAY FROM THE AIRPORT?

Remember that your aircraft is not the only one in the sky. There may be other aircraft that arrived in the area just before yours, and therefore yours is in line to land. Air traffic controllers have to arrange the incoming aircraft, providing safe separation among them and organizing them for landing. Your pilot is merely following the air traffic controller's instructions, which may include passing by the airport and making a few turns before getting aligned with the assigned runway for landing (the pilot always follows the air traffic control instructions). There are also published routes for arrivals at the airport, and if any of these are assigned, we must follow it accurately. In many cases, these arrival routes will make us fly past the airport and make several turns before finally aligning with the landing runway. This high organization is what keeps our skies safe.

I SEE OTHER AIRCRAFT FLYING NEARBY. ISN'T THAT DANGEROUS?

All pilots or airlines, when preparing a flight plan, have to propose an altitude at which they intend to fly. Without exception in the case of commercial flights, this altitude has to be approved by air traffic control authorities. No commercial aircraft can fly at an altitude without being previously approved by the air traffic control facility in control of that particular area. Small private and recreational aircraft face tough restrictions to fly close to a commercial airport served by airlines and are required to be under control by the air traffic control in charge of that area.

As an airline passenger you should not be worried about the proximity of other aircraft because they are all in the screen of the air traffic controllers. In busy airports, it is not one, but several air traffic controllers who are in charge of handling the traffic in the area. Be assured that there is more than one pair of eyes watching over your aircraft and the surrounding ones. Seeing other aircraft flying nearby is fairly common in busy airports while arriving or departing.

I must add that one of the greatest inventions in aviation is called TCAS. Introduced in the 1990s, it is sophisticated electronic equipment that is part of the onboard "transponder," which is the device that allows air traffic controllers to see aircraft on their radar screens. Both are required and mandatory to be operational before a commercial aircraft can be dispatched. TCAS stands for "Traffic Collision Avoidance System" and allows a pilot to see an onboard screen—all the surrounding aircraft that are less than 3,000 feet separated vertically and to a horizontal distance—that depending on equipment, may be from twelve miles up to eighty miles of distance from the aircraft. This device not only allows us to see where other aircraft are located with respect to ours, but will provide an aural warning and a flashing visual warning when another aircraft gets too close to ours, "too close" being as far as five miles. This allows the pilots plenty of time to decide and react. This warning, by the way, is received by both aircraft. On top of that, if the equipment on both aircraft predicts a conflict, it will provide aural and visual guidance on the flight instruments of both aircraft to maneuver. One aircraft will be instructed to climb immediately and the other to descend. In this case, we do not need permission from air traffic controllers since it is a maneuver to avoid a potential collision. It is an accepted practice and only after both aircrafts increase their separation and a conflict no longer exists, we do inform the air traffic controllers. The equipment even includes a voice that says "Clear of conflict" once the situation is resolved.

TCAS has prevented dozens of collisions worldwide, potentially saving tens of thousands of lives. Although collisions are avoided by air traffic controllers in areas where there is radar coverage, they are only human, as we pilots are. For any potential mistake they as controllers and we as pilots can make, TCAS is a great backup for both sides and has saved the day and countless lives many times everywhere in the world. As if aviation wasn't already the safest mode of transportation, after the introduction of TCAS, it is even safer.

WHY IS AVIATION TOUTED AND CONSIDERED THE SAFEST MODE OF TRANSPORTATION?

The aviation industry has controls and mechanisms no other transportation industry has. First of all, we pilots must undergo an initial training for any different type of aircraft we intend to fly and with rare exceptions; we are only allowed to fly one specific model and its variants. If we change jobs or our airline wants to move us to another type of aircraft, once again we start training in that specific type of aircraft and learn how to deal with all potential emergencies in the newly assigned model. Then every six months we have to return to the flight simulator and practice all possible emergencies again. Each and every time we have to pass a practical test in the same simulator to be allowed back into flying.

Also, every six months or every year, depending on the pilot's age, we undergo medical tests by doctors specially authorized for aviation medicals to make sure our vision, hearing, and other health-related issues that could affect our performance are in good order. A heart examination, blood tests, and a physical are part of this exam as well. We are then issued a new medical certificate that certifies we are fit to fly. This certificate, along with our pilot license showing the exact type of airplanes we are certified to fly, are documents we always have to carry with us on every flight.

Air traffic controllers also undergo rigorous training and physical tests. They normally start their careers at small municipal or regional airports where they gain practice and confidence before graduating to the major and bigger airports. Since their job is highly stressful, they must pass psychological exams, and those working in congested airports have a duty time that is normally shorter than in most careers to make sure their mind is fresh and on the job.

As for commercial aircraft, they must be inspected by strictly enforced regulations every specific amount of hours. This is true for the entire aircraft, but particularly for the structure and the engines regardless of how well they may be working.

Aircraft mechanics also have their learning curve, and every job performed must be inspected and signed by a maintenance supervisor. They know they are putting themselves in the line as the rest of all of us involved in the operation of the aircraft, so everybody does his and her job at the highest standard.

All of these in turn go toward your safety while being a passenger in an airliner. You should definitively be more concerned about your safety when riding in a car, where you are much more exposed to an accident than when you ride in an airplane, especially in an airline flight.

Overall, 2011 had the lowest number of aviation fatalities (486) worldwide in the past three years, according to the International Air Transport Association. Most of those fatalities were on smaller general aviation aircraft. The National Transportation Safety Board in the United States analyzed all the airplane accidents between 1983 and 2000. Of the 53,487 people involved, 51,207 survived. That's a survival rate of 95.7 percent. There have also been some reliable calculations that estimate the odds of being in any kind of airplane crash as one in 90 million.

IS THERE A WAY TO HAVE AN IDEA OF HOW MANY AIRCRAFT MAY BE FLYING AT THE SAME TIME?

Just so you can have an idea, at any given time, right this moment as you read this, more than 40,000 airline flights are in the air worldwide, and I strongly believe this number is highly conservative. Consider that in the United States alone, all the major airlines combined have more than 20,000 daily flights. That number, of course, includes departures from every airport within and outside the United States. Now let's go to Europe where the airlines combined may be close to that number and let's do the same for Asia. A smaller number for Australia and Africa means that easily we may be looking at more than 80,000 daily departures worldwide. This is without counting thousands more of executive aircraft and private planes, as well as military planes and all kinds of helicopters sharing the skies with the airliners. It is nothing short of amazing how all these planes take off, land, and share the skies without incident every day as part of the well-greased, regulated, and controlled aviation industry.

If we count as a conservative average, one hundred persons per plane, it means that as you are reading this, more than four million people are flying at this very moment, and again, this number is conservative.

I want to refer you to two of my favorite websites, so you can get the picture of how many airline flights may be flying in an area at a specific time: www.flightradar24.com or www.planefinder.net. Not all areas are covered and not all aircraft are shown due to certain technical requirements. It means that as amazed as you will be when you take a pic at these sites, they are not showing all the aircraft actually flying in that airspace. Still, you will get the picture, especially in high-transit areas like Europe, Asia, and North America. You can even see airplanes flying across the oceans. You will certainly be impressed and hopefully understand, despite the apparent congestion you see, how safe it is to fly. If you put your mouse over a specific plane, it will show you the code for the airline and the flight number. By the way, these websites are also great to track a flight when you are expecting someone to arrive. It will give you an idea of where the plane is, and in other parts of the sites, it will give you its estimated arrival time. I am sure you will enjoy taking a look at them.

WHY DO BIG AIRCRAFT SEEM TO BE POINTING UP WHEN THEY ARE APPROACHING TO LAND?

It's simple. The aircraft is in a controlled descent, helped by the power from the engines. In order to reduce the speed for landing, along with the "flaps," engine power is necessary to prevent the speed from decreasing excessively due to the drag created by the flaps and the landing gear, which contain the aircraft wheels. As you have probably noticed, the wheels or wheels in the nose of the aircraft are small compared with the main wheels below the center of the aircraft. The bigger aircraft may have twelve or more big main wheels in the center while only two small wheels in the front, or as we say, under the nose. No aircraft is designed to be supported by the forward wheel or nose wheels only. It is imperative during landing that the main wheels, which are more numerous and bigger, touch down on the runway first, since these are the wheels designed to support the weight of the aircraft. Later on, the nose wheel comes to the ground to balance the weight and allows steering the aircraft at slow speeds throughout the airport. As you see when an aircraft takes off, the opposite applies; the nose wheels are lifted first off the ground as the aircraft tail is lowered by the "elevators." The rotation for takeoff commences, and the weight rests on the main wheels until the aircraft actually lifts off the ground.

IF ALL THE ENGINES OF AN AIRLINER FAIL IN FLIGHT, CAN IT GLIDE? OR WILL IT UNAVOIDABLY AND IMMEDIATELY FALL TO THE GROUND WITHOUT CONTROL?

<u>**NO, it will not fall to the ground either immediately and uncontrollably, and YES, it can and will glide no matter how big it is.**</u> This is another good one and still a myth for some. Even though the number decreases constantly, there are still some people who swear and affirm that such a big airplane cannot glide. Every aircraft, small or big with two wings can glide. I emphasize with two wings because helicopters are aircraft, and balloons are aircraft, but they do not glide. Helicopter pilots have other techniques they can use if the engine fails, and they will not necessarily fall uncontrollably to the ground. However, that is out of my area of expertise, and I will not elaborate on that. But airplanes are, and I can tell you that every airplane can glide. There is a minimum recommended speed that must be maintained and every commercial pilot is trained in gliding an airplane. It creates time to allow a pilot to try to restart the engines or at least one of them or alternatively find a place to land or "ditch" as necessary. Obviously the lower the altitude of the airplane, the least time the pilot has.

The most recent proof was the excellent job Capt. Sullenberg did when both of the engines of the aircraft under his command were damaged by the ingestion of birds. He did not have much time, but that is when his training, discipline, quick thinking, and experience paid off. As you know, he was able to turn and glide his airliner successfully onto the Hudson River, saving the lives of all on board.

There have been other examples due to volcanic ash, ice crystals or other reasons where all the engines of an aircraft have failed at high altitude, and the pilots had the time to commence a glide and restart all or at least one of the engines and continue the flight to a safe landing. There is a documented case of an airplane that had a fuel leak, and while diverting to an alternative airport, the engines died due to fuel starvation, and the pilots glided the big airplane to a safe landing on the Azores Islands. Everybody survived. For your peace of mind, an aircraft flying at 35,000 feet losing power on all engines has between twenty to thirty minutes of gliding time. With rare exceptions, a pilot can glide the aircraft out of the condition that caused the problem, restart the engines, and continue a safe flight. And yes, commercial-2 engine aircraft can safely fly for hours with just one of the engines.

CAN AN AIRPLANE FLY WITH JUST ONE WING IF IT LOSES THE OTHER IN FLIGHT?

Sounds like a stupid question, but I have been asked it more than once. NO, it cannot fly on just one wing, same as a bird. To your relief, I have no knowledge of an airliner just losing one of its wings in flight.

HOW IS THE AIRCRAFT POWERED ON THE GROUND?

Most commercial airliners have installed an auxiliary power unit (APU) . The aircraft also contains batteries capable of supplying basic power for a limited amount of time. They are used among other things to start the APU. Once it is running, it will recharge the batteries, and at the same time, supply electricity and air conditioning or heating to the aircraft as needed. It is controlled from the cockpit, and in most cases, it is shutdown once the engines are running and take over the electricity and air supply. If the APU is not available while the aircraft is parked at the gate, external air and electricity carts or External Power Units

(EPUs) can be connected to power the aircraft. See definitions for a more detailed explanation.

IS IT SAFE TO FUEL THE AIRCRAFT WHILE PASSENGERS BOARD OR ARE SITTING INSIDE THE AIRPLANE?

It is totally safe. However, just in case, some precautions are taken. You may be asked to turn off your electronic devices and to unfasten your seatbelt in case an evacuation becomes necessary. You will see that the seatbelt sign will be extinguished. Normally it will not be turned ON until fueling is completed.

WHAT IS THE DEAL WITH THE ELECTRONIC DEVICES AFFECTING THE AIRCRAFT SYSTEMS?

It has been determined that the possibility exists that the electromagnetic signals that many of these devices emit may affect sensible instruments in the cockpit. More and more testing is being done, and by the time you are reading this book, it is very likely that more, if not all, of these devices may be allowed at more phases of flight. However, the takeoff and landing are the most critical parts of any flight. Despite what you may be told, I strongly recommend all wireless devices be turned off. Although electronic readers and other devices may be safe with the wireless off, nobody can guarantee that signals will not be emitted. On top of that, many users don't know how to turn the wireless off or may just forget. It is a good idea, just in case, to eliminate potential unsafe emissions and help your safety and that of your fellow passengers by making sure all devices are turned off for takeoff and landing, except maybe those that have no wireless capabilities (provided, of course, they are allowed by current regulations or airline policy). Again, complying with the regulations in place is essential. Ten minutes with your electronic gadgets deactivated will not harm anybody while having them on may subject the aircraft systems to unnecessary and sometimes dangerous interference. Better safe than sorry, don't you think?

WHAT IS THE AGE LIMIT FOR A PILOT TO BE ALLOWED TO FLY?

In 2006, the upper age limit for commercial pilots operating two-pilot aircraft was raised from sixty to sixty-five if the second pilot is younger than sixty. In most countries, the age limit for an airline pilot to be allowed to occupy the position of captain or first officer is now sixty-five. Some countries still have a lower limit. Bear in mind that this limit is for airline pilots. Pilots of privately owned and corporate planes can fly as long as they can get a medical certificate.

HOW DO I KNOW MY PILOTS ARE MEDICALLY FIT TO FLY?

Airline pilots over the age of forty are required to undertake a comprehensive medical test every six months by specially authorized medical doctors specialized in aeronautical medicine. Pilots under forty are required to take this test once a year. In no cases, can the six-month or one-year limitation according to age be exceeded. Of course, like in any other career, this does not guarantee one hundred percent that nothing may happen to the pilot in between tests, but it certainly minimizes the possibilities. The reader may have heard of more than one case where one pilot becomes incapacitated or even dies in flight. Such occurrences are rare but happen and dealing with pilot incapacitation is another important part of any airline pilot training. Even if the captain becomes incapacitated or dies in flight, the first officer is trained to land the aircraft safely. Recently, before this book went to press, there was a well-publicized case in the United States. As stated, the first officer landed the aircraft safely. Obviously, if this happens it is considered an emergency, and the pilot taking charge, even if it is the captain, is required to find the nearest suitable airport and land there.

WHY ARE THERE AT LEAST TWO PILOTS IN THE COCKPIT?

If you read the previous question, that will give you a good part of the answer.

There are some more reasons. Aircraft have different systems that need to be activated and deactivated during normal operation. They also have computers that need to be programmed, and in most cases, some changes are required in flight. At the same time there are checklists to be read, there is the communication with air traffic controllers and there can be abnormal situations to handle. As you can see, especially during "taxi" for takeoff, during and shortly after takeoff, during descent, approach, landing, and taxiing to the gate, the workload is high.

Also, in an abnormal situation, there are procedures to follow and checklists to be read and acted upon. It is imperative in all the previous situations that one pilot devotes his or her full attention to flying the aircraft or continuously monitoring the autopilot operation so safety is not compromised while the other pilot takes care of communication, reading checklists, and operating aircraft systems not related to the actual piloting of the aircraft.

One more additional reason is that two pair of eyes can catch any abnormality faster than just one pair. Continuously monitoring all the aircraft operation and backing each other up by working as a team is key to cockpit safety resulting in overall flight safety.

During long-haul flights, more than a minimum of two pilots are on board, so they can take turns during cruise flight when the workload is low and rest. In the cases of crews augmented this way, the extra or one of the extra pilots—if there is more than one—is required by most airlines to be in the cockpit during takeoff and landing, which are the most demanding parts of any flight and when most incidents and accidents happen. There are international regulations that govern when one or more extra pilots are needed on board based on the expected duration of the flight. In any case, the minimum number is always two.

I USED TO HEAR ABOUT FLIGHT ENGINEERS. WHAT IS A FLIGHT ENGINEER AND WHY DO I RARELY HEAR ABOUT THEM ANYMORE?

Older generation aircraft were less automated than the newer ones. Midsized and larger aircraft have a lot of systems that need to be operated manually, whereas most of these systems operate automatically in newer aircraft. In the same fashion, most of the performance calculations today have more efficient, user-friendly tables or are made through company-provided laptops or onboard, electronic calculation tools. The flight engineer or second officer (as it is also called) is in charge of operating aircraft systems not directly related to the actual flying of the aircraft, but necessary and critical for its operation. The flight engineer's job also was and still is flying in those older airliners, to perform those performance calculations the old fashion way, passing that information on to the pilots, and as stated before, to independently operate aircraft systems, letting the pilots concentrate on flying the airplane.

The flight engineer's panel, where all the information gauges and aircraft system switches are located, is normally behind the pilots and to the right of the aircraft. That is his or her working station, separated from the pilots, but close enough so they can interact between them.

The last aircraft requiring flight engineers were made in the 1980s. Some of them still fly mainly in cargo operations or providing passenger service in third world countries. As long as they are well maintained, they are very reliable machines.

WHERE IS THE SAFEST PLACE TO BE IN AN AIRCRAFT IN CASE OF A CRASH?

In most accidents, the tail is the part that sustains less damage. However, in a recent crash in San Francisco in July 2013, the three fatalities were traveling in the rear of the aircraft. So personally, I do not believe there is a real safer place in an aircraft in case of a crash. People sitting in front, the middle or the rear of an aircraft have been killed and have survived airplane crashes. Fortunately, airline crashes are a rare occurrence, but like car accidents, they will continue to happen. But as stated several times in this book, when talking about transportation, airline travel keeps being by far the safest way of travel. Car crashes happen by the thousands each and every day. We in the aviation industry and particularly in the airline industry strive and aim for years and years of accident free air travel. Having said all that, in my humble opinion, the safest place in an aircraft is any seat with a working seatbelt that you should have fastened as long as you are in your seat and the aircraft is moving in the air or on the ground.

HOW DO PILOTS DEAL WITH STORMS OR BAD WEATHER ENCOUNTERED EN ROUTE?

All aircraft used in commercial transportation have onboard meteorological radar capable of displaying patterns of weather up to 300 miles ahead of the aircraft. We have the capability to reduce that range to shorter distances when getting closer to identify the storm better. The presentation is similar to the ones you see on TV on the weather channel or the weather segment on your local news channel called Doppler radar. In this manner, we inform air traffic controllers that we need to deviate from our route to avoid areas of weather, and in most cases, we avoid the storms flying around them. On the rare occasions when a storm is so wide that it is not possible to circumnavigate it, the onboard radar shows us the less intense areas of it for the few cases when we are forced to penetrate a storm. But most pilots I know, including myself, will do anything in their power to avoid entering a stormy area in the middle of the flight. In some cases when departing or arriving, it may be unavoidable to cross some areas of bad weather, but they are way less intense at low altitudes than they are at high altitudes.

WHAT MIGHT HAPPEN TO AN AIRCRAFT IF IT IS HIT BY LIGHTNING?

Nothing that should create significant concerns. There may be like a momentary flash inside the cabin and even a little bang may be heard, but it will not cause any significant damage that would compromise the safety of the flight. If you can notice, aircraft have at the rear of the wings and in the tail little antennas protruding horizontally towards the back of the aircraft. These are static dischargers, and the electricity absorbed in a lightning situation will be discharged through these little devices and that will be the end of it. It may be a little scary, but that is it. Nothing else will happen.

IS IT SAFER TO FLY IN AN AIRLINE THAN TO FLY IN A CORPORATE AIRCRAFT?

Corporate pilots also have rigorous training programs in which they must demonstrate proficiency in the type of aircraft they fly. I make the note out of respect for my colleagues who work in corporate aviation. They are as trained and as professional as airline pilots. They are just governed by slightly different regulations. Although this book is written mainly for airline passengers, you may have flown or fly someday in a corporate aircraft as a passenger, and this book will serve you well there, too.

Rest assured your corporate pilots have been highly trained and will fly you safely to your destination as well. Some of them used to be airline pilots, and some of them may become airline pilots in the future. It is not uncommon for pilots to change their line of work from corporate to airlines or vice versa.

WHAT WOULD PREVENT A PERSON FROM OPENING ONE OF THE DOORS IN FLIGHT?

No person is strong enough to open an emergency door or one of the main doors mid-flight in a pressurized aircraft. In most passenger planes, the doors open inward. That means that the interior cabin pressure keeps the door sealed shut because it is greater than the exterior pressure while in flight. The more altitude gained, the more pressure differential between the interior and the exterior of the aircraft, and the more pressure keeping the doors closed. Even the doors that open outward have an initial inward movement. The most pressurized the aircraft is, the hardest to move the doors in any direction, since the pressurization practically glues it to its seals until the airplane depressurizes after landing.

WHY DO AIRCRAFT SEEM TO SLOW DOWN EARLY BEFORE ARRIVING AT THE AIRPORT?

As explained in chapter seven, below 10,000 feet is mandatory in most places to fly at a maximum speed of 250 knots, which is equivalent to 288 miles per hour or 460 km/h. This is normally half the speed at which aircraft fly during most of the trip.

One of the reasons is to minimize or avoid altogether any possible damage if a collision with a bird happens. As explained, birds big and small are most likely to be encountered below 10,000 feet. The other reason for slower speeds at low altitudes, since we are talking about that, is because there are more airplanes flying at low altitudes in the vicinity of an airport, including private planes. By reducing speed it is easier for air traffic controllers to manage aircraft flow, and it also provides more time for a pilot to maneuver in case there is a conflict of getting too close to another aircraft.

WHAT ARE THE CLOUDS MADE OF?

A meteorologist would give a detailed scientific explanation. Since my goal is to use simple-to-understand terms let's just say that all clouds are formed by the accumulation of water droplets in the atmosphere. As long as they are lighter than gravity, they will be suspended in the sky. Due to different phenomena, they may become heavier in some cases and come down in the form of light rain, heavy rain, snow, or hail depending on factors in the atmosphere and the temperature of the air through which they fall. They form due to the condensation of water vapor, or in other words, as water vapor—which is initially invisible—climbs in the atmosphere and the temperature becomes lower and lower with altitude. The water vapor starts becoming liquid in the form of tiny water droplets that when clustered together, become visible in different cloud forms depending—as mentioned before—on different atmospheric conditions. So the clouds are basically water transitioning from vapor to liquid.

ABREVIATIONS AND DEFINITIONS

ABBREVIATIONS

ATC: Air Traffic Control
EFC: Expect further clearance
APU: Auxiliary Power Unit
EPU: External Power Unit
ETA: Estimated time of arrival
ETD: Estimated time of departure
ILS: Instrument Landing System
PA: Passenger Address System
SOP: Standard Operating Procedures
TCAS: Traffic Collision Avoidance System

DEFINITIONS:

AIRCRAFT UPSET: An undesirable attitude of the aircraft in flight, something very unlikely to be experienced by an airline passenger. Too many things need to go wrong with the aircraft and the pilots to get to a situation like that. However, rest assured, we airline pilots are trained in flight simulators to deal with that event as well.

AIR SPEED: The speed at which the air hits an object. Whenever you are outdoors standing still and there is wind, that wind has an airspeed at which it's hitting you, even though you are not moving. You hear a lot about wind speed when there are hurricanes or typhoons. This is the speed that we have displayed on our primary speed instruments, except that at high altitudes where the air is less dense, we transition to measure speed in percentage of the sound speed, also known as the Mach number. This differs with the way the speed is measured in a car, which is related to how fast the wheels turn regardless of the wind speed.

AIR TRAFFIC CONTROL: The system in place to control, as its name implies, the aviation traffic in the air and on the ground. It comprises the actual control tower where the controller— most of the time (except in low visibility conditions)—can physically see the airplanes while they roll, takeoff, and land at the airport, and the controllers who maintain communication with the airplanes in flight. These latter controllers, in charge of the radars, are normally in closed quarters with controlled access. They use different radio frequencies depending on the sector the aircraft is flying, and in most cases, they have radar screens where they can see the position, direction, speed, and altitude of the aircraft under their control. Controllers not equipped with radar screens, like in some remote areas, rely on mandatory pilot reports of position and altitude to establish safe separation among aircraft.

AIRWAY: Air routes constructed based on ground radio navigation facilities and on specific coordinates based on the earth circumference, the "equator," and the "meridians." We have charts or maps that show the different airways all over the world. There are even airways for low altitude flights and different ones for high altitude flights. They are normally identified with letters and numbers similar to roads, highways, and motorways. They also contain different positions along them with specific names normally constructed with five letters, as well as the navigation facilities in which ground airways are normally based. Airways in oceanic and non-populated areas are based on GPS navigation, which is based on satellites and GPS or navigation systems on board that help maintain the airway. Since airways are not necessarily a straight line, you may feel the aircraft turning several times during flight. Also, air traffic controllers sometimes, depending on how busy the airspace is, allow flights to take shortcuts, something easy to do in the air which saves fuel and flight time.

ANTI-ICING: The process of applying special liquids to the aircraft exterior to prevent the formation of ice on it ,which may cause a myriad of problems. It is normally applied after a previous operation of de-icing which removes existent ice, snow, or other contaminants using special heated liquids under pressure. Anti-icing is required when precipitation in the form of rain or snow exists or is anticipated in low temperatures.

AUXILIARY POWER UNIT (APU): A turbine type device installed in the aircraft and totally independent from the engines. It is used primarily on the ground to provide electricity and air. It can supply the entire electrical and air conditioning system of the aircraft on the ground. In most aircraft it is usually possible to use it when airborne as a supplemental source of electrical power and air. Except for long flights over water or more than one hour away from a suitable airport in aircraft with two engines, it is not required to be operational for flight.

BANK: Nothing to do with financial institutions here. In aviation terms, bank refers to the inclination of the wings in flight to perform a turn. An airliner will rarely bank more than thirty degrees. For those of you not very familiar with the degrees term, ninety degrees will be if the wings were turned to a point in which they will be totally vertical, one pointing vertically to the earth and one pointing completely to the sky, which, of course, would not allow the aircraft to sustain flight, since the wings would lose all the lift. In case you are wondering, there is a different design and much more powerful engines in military and acrobatic aircraft that allows them, with a properly trained pilot, to accomplish ninety degree banks and other acrobatic maneuvers. However, airliners are not designed to do that.

BLACK BOX: A fire proof, high-impact, resistant container that holds the "voice recorder" and the "flight recorder" which continuously record essential information related to at least the last 30 minutes of a flight to be used in case of the investigation of an aircraft incident or accident.

BRIEFING: A discussion, normally "brief," between crew members during which they introduce each other and discuss previous to the flight the important details: how abnormal situations will be handled, communication codes, flight information and getting integrated to work as a team. There is also normally a briefing between the pilots in the cockpit before departure and another one in the air before starting the descent for arrival.

CROSSWIND: Wind that moves diagonal or perpendicular to a moving object or subject. When it is diagonal, it may contain a headwind or "tailwind" component depending on the direction.

DE-ICING: The process of applying heated water or special approved heated liquids under pressure to the exterior of an aircraft in low temperatures to remove ice, snow, or other contaminants from the airframe. An anti-ice operation may follow if precipitation exists or is anticipated.

DITCH or DITCHING: Landing in water.

EQUATOR: The imaginary line that divides the earth in two parts: the upper part is called the northern hemisphere, and the lower part is called the southern hemisphere. From the equator, up and down, there are ninety imaginary parallel lines up to the poles. They are used to determine what is called "latitude."

EXTERNAL POWER UNIT: As the name implies, it is an external unit that is connected externally to the aircraft to provide electrical power only. Normally a separated, dedicated unit called the air ground cart is needed to be connected to power the air conditioning system or help with the air pressure needed to start the engines if the aircraft APU is not working. There are also external units that can also be connected and supply pre-conditioned or heated air to the aircraft for passenger comfort if the APU is not working.

FLIGHT RECORDER: A device that continuously registers the most important flight parameters, like aircraft altitude, "vertical speed," acceleration, indicated and ground speeds of the aircraft, thrust settings, and engine indications. It is along with the voice recorder part of the called black box.

FLIGHT SIMULATOR: A highly sophisticated, high cost machine that replicates the cockpit of an airplane in exact detail with all switches, indicators, and lights working exactly the way they do on the aircraft. When we sit in the pilot seat of a flight simulator, it is exactly like being seated in the cockpit of the real thing. All switches, lights, and systems work exactly the same as in the real airplane. It is provided with hydraulically and electrically actuated legs that move the device while in operation, replicating the real movements of an aircraft. We can feel acceleration, deceleration, the movement felt during climb and during descent, and even the touchdown on the runway, which like in the real life, may be smooth or not so smooth. It is the best tool in use to train pilots other than the real airplane. The most modern ones generate graphics that show airport runways and environments in extraordinary detail, including day and night scenarios. The flight simulator allows pilot training in all emergency procedures. Even if the pilot crashes the simulator, everybody walks away. Of course, a pilot that cannot perform in the simulator to minimum standards will not be allowed in the cockpit of an airliner.

FUSELAGE: The main body of the aircraft where the cockpit, main cabin, and cargo compartments are located.

GO-AROUND: That is the name given to the maneuver performed to reject the landing. The pilot abandons the approach to the runway and climbs again for different reasons. It is one of the most precious resources and one of the best decisions we pilots can make under different circumstances. It is always performed for a good reason and should not be a concern for the passenger. In chapter five, it is explained in more detail, including the reasons that may cause it.

GROUND SPEED: The speed at which a subject or object moves in reference to the ground. When the moving subject or object is in contact with the ground, the airspeed does not necessarily affect the ground speed except that more effort is required to move against a headwind and less effort is needed to move with a tailwind in comparison to if the wind were zero.

HEADWIND: Wind that moves in the opposite direction of a moving object or subject. For an aircraft in flight, it is the equivalent of a boat navigating in a river upstream.

HOLDING: A racetrack pattern in which the aircraft may have to fly to wait for its time to arrive and land.

JET STREAMS: Air currents in the altitudes that, when shown graphically in a meteorological map, look like rivers. They may be many miles wide and flow normally west to east. Jet streams can reach speeds of more than 200 miles per hour at the highest altitudes over 30,000 feet although the most common range between sixty and one hundred and fifty miles per hour (110 and 270 km/h). They don't cause any real problems, and surprisingly, despite the high speed they can reach, they very rarely cause turbulence. Such high-speed wind, as we all know, is very destructive if experienced on the ground like in tornadoes, hurricanes ,and typhoons. But it is a different story at high altitudes. The main inconvenience is that when an aircraft has to fly against them, it will cause a significant reduction on the ground speed and make the flight longer. To get a better picture, it is as if you are in a boat navigating in a river against the current. But the opposite is true. Flying in the same direction of the jet stream will make the flight shorter, since the aircraft will be pushed by this stream, increasing the real speed about the ground.

On long-haul and transoceanic flights, these currents are taken into consideration, and air routes are retraced daily to take advantage of them or avoid them on upwind flights. Flights flying in the direction of jet streams are routed as close to them as possible. Conversely, flights flying against them are routed as far from them as possible.

The normal speed above the ground for a typical airliner while in cruise flight is around 550 miles per hour or about 900 kilometers per hour in still air. If the flight flies in the direction of the jet stream and let's say the jet stream has an average of one hundred miles per hour, now it will be actually flying over the ground at 650 miles per hour or about 1,050 km/h. The opposite is also true. Flying against the same jet stream will cause the airplane speed above the ground to be 450 miles per hour or about 725 km/h—quite a difference (see ground speed in this section). This will obviously affect the flight time. The longer the flight and the more intense the jet stream, the bigger the difference. That is why, for example, a flight from East Asia to the North American west coast may take nine hours while the same flight from the North American west coast to East Asia may take fourteen, or a flight from

Europe to the North American east coast may take nine hours westbound, but only seven hours eastbound.

It is worth mentioning that these jet streams are virtually nonexistent towards the poles. That is why in polar flights, for example, from east North America to Asia and vice versa, the time difference in flight duration is not as noticeable.

KNOT or KNOTS: It is equivalent to what is called a nautical mile. Speed on aircraft and on ships is measured in knots. One knot equals 1.15 miles per hour or 1.85 km/h. In the case of aircraft, as the airplane climbs and the air becomes less dense, the speed is more accurately measured on the percentage of the speed of sound, also called the Mach Number.

LANDING GEAR: The components of an aircraft that contain the wheels and serve the double purpose of supporting the weight of the airplane on the ground and providing mobility through the installed wheels. All commercial airliners contain one main landing gear on each side and a nose landing gear in the front that provides steering. Some of the biggest airliners have steerable wheels as well on the main landing gears. One of the most revered airliners of the old times, which had a military version as well, the DC-3, had a tail gear instead of a nose gear.

LATITUDE: A measure north or south of the equator to determine the exact position of something or somebody. It is used in aviation to report the position of an aircraft especially when flying over the ocean or unpopulated areas. It is also used by the maritime industry for the same purpose with ships. These days, with the extended use of GPS, it is even easier to pinpoint a position using latitude and "longitude." By intersecting latitudes with longitudes, it is possible to determine the exact position of anything on earth. Each one of these lines is called a degree and has other smaller units in between, same as with longitude.

LEG: We call every portion of the flight between a takeoff and a landing a leg or "sector."

LONGITUDE: It is similar to the latitude but now cutting the earth with imaginary vertical lines. The zero line also called the prime meridian or Greenwich meridian goes through the United Kingdom and parts of West Africa. Any position to the right or east of this imaginary line is called longitude east and to the left is called longitude west. In this case, one hundred and eighty imaginary lines are drawn to each side of the prime meridian. By intersecting latitudes with longitudes it is possible to determine the exact position of anything on earth. Each one of these lines is called a degree and has other smaller units in between, same as with latitude.

LONG-HAUL FLIGHT: Although there is no specific definition, a long-haul flight is normally considered any flight that lasts more than nine hours from takeoff until landing. These flights require one or two additional pilots to the minimum two normally required to allow for rest periods. The longest passenger flights in regular service go about eighteen hours. The most common long-haul flights last between nine and sixteen hours.

MACH NUMBER: In simple terms, it is the speed relative to the speed of sound. Mach 1 equals the speed of sound. At high altitudes, aircraft speed is measured and reported in percentage of the Mach number. Most airliners during cruise fly at speeds between Mach 0.74 to Mach 0.86 which is between seventy-four percent and eighty-six percent of the speed of sound. Some advanced business jets reach speeds of Mach 0.90 or ninety percent the speed of sound. The well remembered and sadly now defunct Concorde used to fly at Mach 2 or twice the speed of sound.

MAXIMUM CERTIFIED TAKEOFF WEIGHT: The maximum weight at which an aircraft can safely takeoff and continue to fly to a safe landing even if one of its engines fails on takeoff. This weight is affected by several factors and cannot always be used. Variables like temperature, airport altitude, condition of the runway, and others of technical nature require an adjustment, limiting the maximum weight with which an aircraft can be loaded.

MERIDIANS: Imaginary vertical lines drawn from the North Pole to the South Pole. Three hundred and sixty of them are used equivalent to the 360 degrees of the circumference of the earth and are used to determine the position of a craft. See "longitude."

NOSE (OF THE AIRCRAFT): The front of the aircraft, including the area where the cockpit is located.

PITCH: The inclination of the main fuselage in relation to the horizon measured in degrees. Zero degrees is when the aircraft is leveled on the ground and close to zero when in cruise, with some technical small variables not necessary to mention here. Ninety degrees would be if the fuselage is completely vertical, which of course should never happen. During takeoff, normal pitch up is between fifteen to twenty degrees. During descent, normal pitch down is between five to ten degrees.

RUNWAY: A long, paved, wide surface at the airport intended for airplanes to accelerate and takeoff and to land and decelerate after a flight. Big airports have big, long, wide runways while small municipal airports have shorter, narrower runways designed for the operation of smaller aircraft. Many airports have more than one runway, in some cases with different orientation and in some others with parallel orientation. Therefore, it is not uncommon when approaching to land, to see another aircraft nearby, flying parallel to yours. It is normal, and it just means your aircraft is landing at a runway while the other is landing in a parallel runway. Both pilots are informed by air traffic control about the other aircraft and air traffic controllers at the same time maintain a close watch so there are no surprises. Where approved, it is completely safe. There are airports with as many as six different runways. With very rare exceptions, since aircraft should take off and land against the wind, the runway may be used in either direction, depending on the direction the wind is blowing. Air traffic controllers and airport authorities determine which runways will be used. For safety and efficiency of operations, some airports may designate a specific runway for landings only while another for takeoffs only at certain times of the day.

SECTOR: We call every portion of the flight between a takeoff and a landing a sector or "leg."

STALL: Loss of lift on the wings due to the speed being slower than the minimum required to sustain flight or due to an unusual attitude of the aircraft. It is appropriate to mention that airplanes have a limit in the inclination of the wings when making a turn (see "bank" in this section). After a certain degree of inclination, the flow of air on the wings is disturbed, requiring a higher minimum speed to maintain the lift. The same applies to the inclination of the aircraft to climb or descend. If the inclination or pitch to climb is too high, the wings will lose lift due to the angle exceeding the designed maximum angle, and that in turn will also cause the loss of speed. Conversely, if the "pitch down" or "nose down" of the aircraft is beyond the certified limitation, despite the increase of speed, the wings will no longer be able to sustain controlled flight and that would cause the aircraft to fall out of control. Fortunately, most aircraft are designed in a way that they tend to oppose themselves to these undesirable attitudes. The most modern aircraft incorporate automatic systems that will warn and even assist the pilot in correcting any of these undesirable situations. Only during test flights or in flight simulators are these maneuvers performed deliberately, and we pilots are trained in flight simulators on how to respond to any of these situations called "aircraft upset."

TAILWIND: Wind that moves in the same direction of a moving object or subject. For an aircraft in flight, it is the equivalent of a boat navigating in a river downstream.

TAIL OF THE AIRCRAFT: As the name implies, it comprises the rearmost section of an airplane.

TAXI: Taxiing an aircraft means driving it on the ground. Most aircraft have either a steering wheel or a tiller on the captain's side that will move the little wheels on the nose to steer the aircraft on the ground. Some of the big late model aircraft have also a tiller on the copilot's side.

TAXIWAY: That is the name received by the areas of pavement or equivalent to the streets in an airport designed for use by airplanes to move about the airport from the gates to the runways for takeoff and from the runways to the gates after landing.

Traffic Collision Avoidance System (TCAS): Equipment on board the aircraft that works like a radar, detecting and showing to the pilot on a screen all the surrounding aircraft less than 3,000 feet separated vertically and to a horizontal distance that depending on equipment, may be from twelve miles up to eighty miles of distance from the aircraft. It is now mandatory on all commercial aircraft used by the airlines and passenger aircraft used in corporate aviation. It will issue maneuver commands to two aircraft in potential conflicting paths, effectively separating them, provided of course the pilots of both aircraft follow the commands. Before it happens, though, pilots are able to notice the position of each other's aircraft on an onboard screen and know what to expect, so on the rare occasions, electronic commands are issued—they are a last resort measure. When two aircraft are predicted to be in a conflicting path, a visual and aural warning is received in the cockpit. It is called a "Traffic Advisory." It creates awareness of the proximity of both aircraft, and pilots may decide to maneuver on their own to avoid conflict, alert the other aircraft by turning on exterior lights, or both. If the conflict is not resolved in this manner, then as a last resort, the system will order one aircraft to climb and the other to descend to separate their paths. This is called a "Resolution Advisory," and it is of immediate mandatory compliance for all pilots. Thousands of potential collisions have been prevented and dozens totally avoided thanks to this wonderful equipment.

TEST FLIGHT: Every commercial airplane built before delivery to the client company or airline must undergo several tests on the ground and then in flight. These test flights are performed by specially trained pilots. The aircraft is pushed to its limits and placed in situations not normally encountered in a regular flight. The aircraft must satisfactorily pass all these test flights and its structure and components revised again after each one of these flights to make sure it is in perfect condition. Upon delivery, designated pilots from the client company or airline will also perform what is called an acceptance flight, where they fly the airplane and verify that everything is in perfect working order. If there is something wrong, they will not take delivery of the aircraft until they are satisfied it is in top-notch condition. Only then will they fly it to the company base where it will start commercial service.

THRUST REVERSERS: A system on the engines that directs the airflow, meaning the thrust of the engines forward of the aircraft instead of backward. It is used after landing to help reduce the speed of the aircraft. For safety reasons, as you can imagine, it is locked when the aircraft is in flight. There are sensors on the wheels that must sense the weight of the aircraft is on the wheels to allow the use of thrust reversers.

TRANSPONDER: An onboard electronic device that transmits a radio signal. This signal is picked up by air traffic control radars and allows a clear view on the controller radar screen of the aircraft position, direction, and altitude. They can see the flight number as well. This allows the controllers to manage air traffic and insures proper separation between aircrafts. It incorporate the TCAS as well allowing other pilots of nearby aircraft see on an onboard screen the position, direction, and altitude of nearby aircraft, thereby enhancing the security and preventing potential collisions. It's an excellent backup system for us as pilots and for the controllers as well, and no commercial aircraft is allowed to dispatch if the transponder is not functioning properly. Likewise, all private aircraft operating in certain busy areas or next to commercial airports must have one in good working order.

VERTICAL SPEED: The rate at which an aircraft climbs or descends. It is measured in feet per minute. Normal rates of climb for most airliners go from about 4,000 feet per minute at low altitude to about 1,000 feet per minute at high altitudes. The closer to the maximum altitude an aircraft can climb at a given weight, the lower the rate of climb. Typical rates of descent are between 2,000 to 3,000 feet per minute, which can be increased up to 6,000 feet per minute if needed using the speed brakes or spoilers, those little panels over the wings previously described. At low altitudes rates of descent are lower and the normal rate of descent during final approach to the runway is about 700 feet per minute, reduced, of course, to the minimum shortly before landing.

VOICE RECORDER: A device that continuously records all conversations in the cockpit as long as at least one of the engines is running. It normally erases everything but the last 30 minutes of conversation, which will be critical to know in case of an abnormal situation. It, along with the flight recorder, is part of the black box.

WINDSHEAR: A rapid change in wind direction and/or velocity associated with nearby storms that may affect the handling of the aircraft at the low speeds used for approach and landing or for takeoff. Pilots are alerted to its presence by air traffic controllers who may get the information on their instruments that measure the wind, from reports from other pilots, or by onboard detectors that generate a light and aural warning onboard in advance. There are specific procedures to follow and maneuvers to perform in areas of known windshear or if the aircraft becomes affected by this phenomenon.